Living a
LIFE
You LOVE

EMBRACING THE ADVENTURE OF BEING
LED BY THE HOLY SPIRIT

JOYCE MEYER

LARGE **PRINT**

FaithWords
Hachette Book Group
1290 Avenue of the Americas, New York, NY 10104
faithwords.com
twitter.com/faithwords

First Edition: April 2018

FaithWords is a division of Hachette Book Group, Inc.
The FaithWords name and logo are trademarks of Hachette Book Group, Inc.

The publisher is not responsible for websites (or their content)
that are not owned by the publisher.

The Hachette Speakers Bureau provides a wide range of authors for speaking events.
To find out more, go to www.hachettespeakersbureau.com or call (866) 376-6591.

Library of Congress Cataloging-in-Publication Data has been applied for.

ISBNs: 978-1-4555-6016-5 (hardcover), 978-1-4555-6020-2 (large type), 978-1-4555-6018-9 (ebook), 978-1-5460-1026-5 (international)

Printed in the United States of America

LSC-C

10 9 8 7 6 5 4 3 2 1

Be so busy loving your life that you have no time for hate, fear, or regret.

Author unknown

CONTENTS

INTRODUCTION

What do you love? I mean . . . *really* love?

If you're like most people, you may say, "I love my family," "I love my spouse, my friends, my church," or even "I love the Lord." And then there are the more temporal things we all enjoy, like, "I love my house," "I love a good dinner at a nice restaurant," "I love a great cup of coffee," "I love to go shopping," and "I certainly love a well-timed vacation."

These are all great things and make perfectly reasonable answers. We love and appreciate the people and things in our lives that bring a measure of contentment and happiness.

But I've discovered that very few people would answer, "Joyce, I absolutely *love* my life." Most of us are more frustrated with our lives than we are at peace with them. Very few people live lives full of joy, excited to wake up each day, and filled with wonder at what God might do next. I believe a good question for all of us to ask ourselves is, "Am I merely enduring my life, trying to make it through each day, or do I truly love it?"

If you don't love your life, then you should do something to change it. It may require a change of attitude or perspective. It may require getting a new career or even moving to a new city, and it may require getting some new friends and learning to see yourself the way God does. There are things we can do to ensure that we will love our life. After all, we only get one life, and we should love it and live it with enthusiasm and zeal.

I want to mention a very important thing right here in the beginning, and that is that we should never compare our life with anyone else's, because doing so often causes us to not love our own life fully and joyfully. It is "your" life that I want to teach you to love. It is the only one you have, and God will not give you anyone else's, so how about taking what you've been given and doing the most you can with it?

The daily grind often wears us down. The bills pile up, the calendar gets too full, the diet doesn't seem to be working, the traffic is infuriating, the doctor's report is troubling, the children are not behaving, the job is exhausting—and to top it all off, that darn kitchen faucet is dripping again!

These irritations (and so many others just like them) too often cause us to survive life rather than actually enjoy it. I can picture many of you nodding along in agreement as you read these words…life can be challenging, to say the least. But everyone's life is challenging in some way at times, and that is why wanting someone else's life is pointless. You may find that it is easier to deal with your problems than it would be to deal with theirs.

But you can become a person who says: *"I love my life."* We can face challenges, deal with frustrations, have less than pleasurable circumstances, and still love our lives.

I think about the examples we see in the Bible:

- David dealt with giants, opposing armies and a father who favored his brothers over him, and yet he wrote: "You will show me the path of life; in Your presence is fullness of joy; in Your right hand there are pleasures forevermore" (Psalm 16:11).
- Solomon had the pressures of building the Temple and running a kingdom, and yet he said: "Every man should eat and drink and see and enjoy the good of all his labor—it is the gift of God" (Ecclesiastes 3:13).
- The apostle Paul faced shipwrecks, a physical ailment, constant criticism, and persecution, but he told us: "I have learned to be content [and self-sufficient through Christ, satisfied to the point where I am not disturbed or uneasy]

regardless of my circumstances" (Philippians 4:11).

- Mary would give birth in a barn after traveling in extreme conditions, and yet she said: "From now on all generations will count me blessed and happy and favored by God!" (Luke 1:48).

These men and women faced difficulty, challenges, opposition, and frustrations at various times, but they were able to look past that and live lives full of joy and contentment—they learned the secret of loving their lives!

What I want to share with you in the pages of this book has come from years of personal Bible study and *lots* of personal experience. You see, there was a time in my life when I lived stuck in frustration, anger, and insecurity. Because of the abuse I endured at the hands of my father as a child, I had many issues to work through as an adult. I had anger problems, I was easily discouraged, I compared myself to people around me, and I drove myself to the point of exhaustion trying to accomplish my goals. I loved God, I loved teaching His Word and I loved my friends and family, but I couldn't really say I loved my life. I continually wanted and searched for an elusive "something else" that I thought would satisfy the longing in my soul, but somehow it always evaded me.

But God has taught me so much over the years. It wasn't always easy—I certainly made my fair share of mistakes along the way—but I can confidently say today that I love the life God has given me. I don't love it because it is perfect, but because it is a gift from God.

The truth is that God has given you a wonderful, joy-filled, overcoming life, too...you just need to discover it. And I think this book will go a long way in helping you do that. The life that we have currently is the only one that we have, and disliking it won't change it. If God leads you to change something that will help you enjoy it more, then by all means do so, but if not, then it is time to embrace your life and learn to love it!

In the chapters to come, I hope to challenge and equip you with the tools you need to have a life you can love. Some things will be a reminder of what God has already shown you, but many of the things we'll discuss will be new, thought-provoking steps to take in your spiritual journey. For example, in the pages to come, you'll discover that...

- You can't live a life that you love unless love is the central theme of your life.
- Your attitude affects your life more than any outside circumstance ever will.

- Each new day is more than just another day of the week; it's a new opportunity, a new beginning, and you can live with an attitude of expectation.
- You should start doing things that you have always wanted to do but kept putting off until another time.
- Celebrating your victories and progress, no matter how small, is God's will for you.

And so much more!

If you are ready to begin living with a whole new attitude, overcome your obstacles, and wake up looking forward to the day rather than dreading it, keep reading. This is going to be a book that you'll want to read time and time again. And when it's all said and done, I believe you're going to be able to declare once and for all, *I love the life GOD has given me!*

SECTION I

"Loving Life Begins with Loving God"

And Jesus replied to him, "You shall love the Lord your God with all your heart, and with all your soul, and with all your mind."

Matthew 22:37

CHAPTER 1

God Has an Amazing Plan for You

Never be afraid to trust an unknown future to a known God.

Corrie ten Boom

We're all planners by nature. It's just a part of who we are as humans—we want to know what the plan is. *What direction should I take in life? How are things going to turn out?* Or perhaps smaller things like, *What should I make for dinner tonight?* or *What should I wear to the company Christmas party?* Big plans or little plans, down the road or later on today—on some level, we are all planners.

Now, some people are more serious about it than others. For example, there are those people who have mapped out the next ten years of their lives in great detail. They know exactly what career path they are aiming for, what type of house they want to build, and how many kids they are going to have. Their investment plans are working for them and their relationship goals are right on schedule. Nothing is left to chance. After all, they've got plans!

And then there are others who are a little more flexible. Sure, they plan, but a week or two, or at the most a year is about as far as they've looked. These people have hopes and dreams just like everyone else, but they haven't exactly put them on a timetable. They're more casual and laid-back. The budget is simply a guideline, the career will work itself out, and their plans could easily be titled: "Let's Wait and See What Happens."

Whether you're a long-term planner or a short-term planner, I want to share a word of caution with you today: Your plan is flawed. No matter how long you've worked on it, no matter how foolproof it seems, there is only so much happiness *your* plan can bring you.

You see, the problem with making our own plans is there are human limitations that we all face. We don't know what's going to come our way next week, much less next year. We don't know what challenges or opportunities we are going to come across. We don't know what decisions the people around us are going to make, and we don't know how the world will change in the years to come.

Many variables can alter our plans. In all honesty, we don't even know if we'll want the same thing two years from now. You've changed your mind before; who's to say you won't change it again? Your career goals could change, you may need to take on a responsibility that you were not planning on, your financial obligations could shift...transition is a part of life.

Now, don't get me wrong, I'm not saying it's wrong to have a plan. In fact, it is very wise to have a budget, an appointment calendar, and an idea of where you are going in the future. I've often heard it said: "Plan ahead. It was not raining when Noah started building the ark." So, planning, in and of itself, is not a bad thing. But here is what I want you to see...

It is only when you submit your plan to God that you can begin to love your life.

The best your plan will ever be able to do is make life tolerable, but living in the plan God has for you is the key to loving every single day of your life. Your plan may be good, but God's plan is great. Your plan may bring *some* happiness, but God's plan brings overflowing joy. Your plan may pay the bills, but God's plan brings true and lasting success.

> It is only when you submit your plan to God that you can begin to love your life.

If you're ready to move from surviving life and really begin to love the life you have, the first thing you need to recognize is this...

God's Plan Is Better Than Yours!

I think one of the most encouraging things about being a Christian is knowing that God sees the end of everything from the beginning, and nothing we go through is a surprise to Him. He's not wringing His hands, wondering how to get us through each day. He's omniscient (all-knowing) and omnipotent (all-powerful), and He has a plan in place for our future.

Anytime you are tempted to get worried or anxious, thinking, *Are things going to work out? How am I going to get through this situation? Where is God when I need Him?* (all questions that steal our joy and our love for life)—just remember what the Word of God has to say:

> And we know [with great confidence] that God [who is deeply concerned about us] causes all things to work together [as a plan] for good for those who love God.
>
> Romans 8:28

> We receive from Him whatever we ask because we [carefully and consistently] keep His commandments and do the things that are pleasing in His sight [habitually seeking to follow His plan for us].
>
> 1 John 3:22

God-of-the-Angel-Armies has planned it.
Who could ever cancel such plans? His is
the hand that's reached out. Who could
brush it aside?

Isaiah 14:27 (MSG)

What an encouragement! Not only does God have
a plan, but there is no one who can "brush it aside."
If we will simply trust Him and submit to His plan,
there is no enemy or obstacle that can keep God's
purposes from coming to pass.

Never forget: Regardless of the situation or out-
ward appearance, God has a plan for your life, and
He is faithfully putting His
plan into place. When you
realize God is in control, it
takes all the pressure off. You
don't have to worry or fret,

> When you realize God is
> in control, it takes all the
> pressure off.

thinking, *How am I going to fix this situation?* You can
simply rest in the fact that God has it all planned out.
We should all do what God asks us to do and then
trust Him to do what we cannot do! We can embrace
the great adventure of being led by the Holy Spirit
and trust that He will lead us day by day into the perfect plan our Father has for us.

A friend of mine told me recently about a day he
spent surprising his two children. Knowing they were

going to hang out for the afternoon, the kids asked if they could go to the park and maybe stop for an ice cream after—this was their plan. But little did they know that my friend had been making plans, too.

He did take them to the park and for an ice cream...but this was just the beginning. He told me, "Joyce, we don't do it often, but my wife and I just wanted to spoil them for the day." So from there they went to the movies, out for dinner at the kids' favorite restaurant, and then a trip to the local arcade to top off the night. (Wow, I wish I could have gone!)

The point is simple: The kids had a plan, but their parents had a plan also, and theirs was much better than anything the kids could have imagined. My friend and his wife had been planning the day all along. They had everything under control. They knew how much it would cost, how to get to their destinations, what movie the kids would love, and how to make it all happen. And they knew the kids would love it!

That's how God is with you. He's been planning your life all along. Nothing is left to chance, and you are not on your own. God is carefully working His plan. He knows where to take you, and the exact right time to do it. He knows what you need to succeed. And you know what? He knows you're going to love it!

The key is for us to learn to cooperate with God's plan. Rather than stubbornly hold on to our plans, we would be wise to discover His plan and then obey God as He guides us. That's precisely what Ephesians 2:10 tells us to do. The apostle Paul writes that we should "walk" in God's plan, "living the good life which He prearranged and made ready for us" to live. And the "good life" leads me to something so encouraging to remember...

More Than You Can Imagine

Many times, when people hear that God has a plan for their lives, they become hesitant. They assume God is going to ask them to do something that will be difficult and sacrificial, and they won't like it. The reason why many people don't choose to believe in God is because they view Him as a hard taskmaster; they think they won't have any fun, and life will be dull and boring. That could not be further from the truth. "Doing life" with God is a grand adventure!

The plan God has for you isn't some sort of spiritual hard labor. God is not in the arm-twisting business. He isn't going to force you to go somewhere or do something unless He has first put that desire in your heart. God wants to set you in a place—whether it's a family, a home, a career, a calling—that you can love and enjoy. Sure, there will be challenges from time to time, but you'll know you're living the life of your dreams.

First and foremost, God has laid out a path for your spiritual fulfillment. His plan is for you to be redeemed from sin and guilt, made right with Him, and have peace in your soul. This is the very foundation of your life. But God's plan goes beyond the inner life. The truth is that God wants you to enjoy your life every day. That's why Jesus said in John 10:10: "I came that they may have and enjoy life, and have it in abundance [to the full, till it overflows]."

Those words from Jesus are so encouraging and important—learning to love your life is a biblical principle! There is nothing more scriptural than knowing that God's plan for your life is far greater than your plan.

Ephesians 3:20 says it this way:

> Now to Him who is able to [carry out His purpose and] do superabundantly more than all that we dare ask or think [infinitely beyond our greatest prayers, hopes, or dreams], according to His power that is at work within us…

And 1 Corinthians 2:9 says:

> But just as it is written [in Scripture], Things which the eye has not seen and the ear has not heard, and which have not entered into the heart of man, all that God has prepared for those who love Him [who hold Him in affectionate reverence, who obey Him, and who gratefully recognize the benefits that He has bestowed].

These are promises you can build your entire life around. When you submit your plans to God, He can do things that are "infinitely beyond our greatest prayers, hopes, or dreams." Just as we love to surprise

> Learning to love your life is a biblical principle!

our children, God loves to surprise us with things beyond our most daring expectations, and believing that is one of the main ingredients in living a life that you can love. I encourage you to expect to be amazed by the goodness of God!

I think about the life of David. When we first read about David in 1 Samuel 16, he is merely a shepherd boy. He's out in the fields, tending his father's sheep. I wonder what the plans were for his life. Maybe he was hoping to one day take over the family sheep business, or maybe he was considering joining the army like his older brothers at some point in time. Because of his family limitations (David was the youngest of seven brothers) and his predicament (a lowly shepherd), David may have had some very modest plans for his life.

But God had plans that were greater than anything David could imagine.

You probably know the story well. At God's urging, the prophet Samuel showed up and anointed David the next king of Israel. David would go on to defeat Goliath, lead the army, play music before King Saul, become best friends with the prince, Jonathan, and eventually become king himself. What a life! I'm sure David would be the first one to proclaim, *God's plans were far better than anything I could have even imagined!*

> I encourage you to expect to be amazed by the goodness of God!

And David isn't the only example. Joseph went from a prison to the palace (Genesis 37–41). Gideon was hiding in a cave, but God used him to lead a nation (Judges 6–8). Esther was a captive who became a queen (Esther 2). And Peter was a fisherman whom God transformed into a pillar of the early church. Each one of these men and women saw their lives veer from the plans they had made...but God had much better plans in store.

As you read these words, I want you to know that the very same principle is true for you. The plans you have made for your life may be very good, but God's plans are better. He may take your plans and add more to them, or He may have a totally different plan for you all together, but you can always be sure that He has your best interest in mind. His plan will never be burdensome. It will always be something that fulfills the very desires He has placed in your heart. And it is guaranteed to be something far greater than what you could have imagined on your own.

But What If I Don't See Anything Happening?

A life filled with peace is a life you can truly love. If you can be at peace when the economy drops, if you can be at peace when the job pressures rise, if you can be at peace when the kids or grandkids are driving you crazy...then your life is a joy rather than a chore.

I believe the key to living with peace is trusting God's plan even before you see the results.

You see, God's plan in your life doesn't happen overnight—it's a process. He is building your faith, healing your soul, refreshing your spirit all in due time. You won't always see (or understand) exactly what God is doing, but you can always be sure He is at work. That's why Philippians 1:6 promises that God "who has begun a good work in you will [continue to] perfect and complete it until the day of Christ Jesus [the time of His return]." Just because you can't yet see what God is doing doesn't mean He isn't doing something great.

> I believe the key to living with peace is trusting God's plan even before you see the results.

John Flavel once said, "The providence of God is like Hebrew words—it can be read only backwards."[1] I really like this quote. There are some things in our lives we can understand only when we look back on them. In the middle of a trial, it's often too hectic to fully understand what God's plan might be, but when you get on the other side of it, you can look back and comprehend what God was accomplishing in you and for you through it all.

So let me ask you a question: What are you going through today that is causing you to worry, be anxious, or be afraid? Is there an obstacle or a difficulty that is stealing your joy and causing you to dread your day instead of loving your life?

Well, whatever it is that has come to your mind, I want to encourage you to cast that care at the feet of Jesus. Instead of focusing on the problem, rest in peace, knowing that He has the solution. You may not see it yet, but God is working on your behalf, and if you'll trust Him, there will come a time when you'll look back on this situation and realize all God did to bring you through.

You can love your life when you realize it is not your own (1 Corinthians 6:19–20). God is in control; He has a great plan. That is something you can get excited about!

Don't Forget…

- It is only when you submit your plan to God that you can begin to love your life.
- Not only does God have a plan for your life, but there is no one who can "brush it aside."
- When you submit your plans to God, He can do things that are "infinitely beyond our greatest prayers, hopes, or dreams" (Ephesians 3:20).
- When you decide to trust God's plan rather than rely on your own, peace is the natural result.

To live is the rarest thing
in the world. Most
people exist, that is all.

Oscar Wilde

CHAPTER 2

"This Moment Is the Most Important One You Have"

Forever is composed of nows.

Emily Dickinson

Imagine with me if your bank made some new policies regarding your personal checking account. *Get ready, you're going to like these changes!* The new policies go something like this:

1. Every single day, you get $86,400 deposited into your account. It's all yours. You can spend it as you see fit.
2. However, each night, the bank cancels any money you didn't use that day. *Nothing* carries over to the next day.

Sounds pretty good, right?

What would you do? I know what I would do. I'd go about each day spending that money as wisely as possible. I'd invest it, I'd share it with others, and I'd spend it on things that really matter. (And I'd probably do some serious shopping, too!) With an opportunity like that in front of me, I'd make the most of each dollar, maximizing the opportunity every day.

I ask you to think about that because, believe it or not, you have been given a similar policy, but not with money—with time. Each day you are given 86,400 brand-new seconds to spend however you want. Isn't that amazing to consider? But here is the catch: None of that time carries over to the next day. It has to be lived in the present. Yesterday is over; tomorrow is not promised; you've got 86,400 seconds to spend today.

> *Each day you are given 86,400 brand-new seconds to spend however you want.*

I want to suggest that you stop wasting time being negative. For example, ask God to help you get the word "hate" out of your vocabulary. Start paying attention to how much people use that phrase, and you will get an insight into why some days seem so distasteful. We hear and say things like, "I hate driving in traffic every day to get to work," "I hate the weather in my city" (I have been guilty of saying this one a lot lately), "I hate doing laundry, or cleaning house, or cutting the grass, or waiting in the doctor's office," and thousands of other things. It's really harmful when we think or say that we hate certain people or that we hate ourselves. But we can learn to love our lives by speaking more *love language* in our day and getting rid of the *hate language*.

Each day is a new opportunity, and you should avoid focusing on the things you don't like and perhaps even dread. It is possible to do something that maybe isn't your favorite thing to do and still not hate it. You don't have to live regretting the past or dreading the future—you can maximize the 86,400 seconds God has given you today. This is more than just a good idea; it's a biblical principle. Ephesians 5:16 says, "Making the very most of your time [on Earth, recognizing and taking advantage of each opportunity and using it with wisdom and diligence]," and Psalm 118:24 says, "This . . . is the day which the Lord has made; let us rejoice and be glad in it."

Let us rejoice and be glad in it . . . hmmm. Is this a proper description of how you and I go about each day? Or would it be more accurate to say, *Let us stew and be mad in it?* or *Let us sulk and be sad in it?* Too often, this is the case. Rather than rejoicing in the new day God has given us, we are letting precious time slip by while we grumble, complain, regret, worry, or give in to fear.

If you want to love your life, it's time to make a change. You have only one life on this side of eternity; it would be a tragedy to waste it. Today could be the day you begin making the most of your time and maximizing every moment.

Three Ways to Maximize the Moment

When I say that we can love and enjoy our lives, I realize that every day isn't summer vacation and parties. We still have jobs to go to, children to raise, deadlines to make, and responsibilities to meet.

But the obligations of daily living don't have to steal your joy. You can learn to enjoy the moment even when that moment involves going to the grocery store or cleaning the house. It's all about choosing to see the blessings of God and the good in each day. Loving your life isn't something that happens by accident. It is a result of healthy, biblical choices that you make on a daily basis. Let me show you three choices you can begin making today that will help you maximize the moments God gives you.

1. Obey in the Moment

Obedience may not be the first thing that comes to your mind when talking about *loving your life* and *maximizing the moment*, but being obedient to God is one of the best ways to live a joyful, overcoming life. That's why the Bible tells us: "To obey is better than sacrifice" (1 Samuel 15:22).

Better for whom? It's better for you!

When you learn to obey God's Word and the leading of His Holy Spirit the very moment He instructs you to do something, you'll be amazed at how much more enjoyable your life becomes. You will be more peaceful

> Loving your life isn't something that happens by accident. It is a result of healthy, biblical choices that you make on a daily basis.

and fulfilled knowing that you are in the will of God. Nothing is more uncomfortable than a guilty conscience due to knowingly disobeying God.

One thing that helps us truly love our lives is when we let God work through us to help other people. All we need to do is be willing to obey God by following the gentle nudges from the Holy Spirit, and it adds a quality of enthusiasm to our life that is truly inspiring. Let me give you an example of how obeying God in the moment can affect you:

Recently, I was buying a cup of coffee in a local coffee shop. The barista and I were chatting as I paid for my coffee, and somehow the coffeemaker the store had on display came up in conversation. It was a very nice coffeemaker, and the young barista said,

"I'm saving up my money because I *really* want to buy that coffeemaker one day."

As soon as she said those words, I felt the leading of the Lord to buy that coffeemaker for her. There was no audible voice from Heaven or anything like that; I just knew in my spirit that God was telling me to bless this young lady. So that's what I did. I bought that coffeemaker as a gift and told her, "I just want to bless you with this."

Now, let me tell you, she was overjoyed. She thanked me profusely and said that no one had ever done anything like that for her. But as happy as she was, I think I was even happier. It was such a special moment, and it brought so much enjoyment to my day.

God knew exactly what that barista needed... and He knew exactly what I needed that day. We both walked away with joy in our hearts and a wonderful experience to thank God for.

Then later that day I saw the young lady in a restroom in the shopping mall and she asked me, "Why were you so nice to me?" I told her that God loved her and wanted her to be blessed. That was when she shared that her mother had died with cancer, and that she had been angry with God; she felt that even if He did exist, He didn't love her. I had an opportunity to briefly share the truth about His love with her, and after giving the incident some thought I realized that the coffeepot was merely used to open the girl's heart so God could show her that He did indeed care about her. At that point my joy doubled, because God had allowed me to participate in such an amazing, divinely appointed event.

But here's the thing: I would have missed that moment if I had not been obedient to God. If I had thought, *I can't do that. That coffeemaker is too expensive,* or *This is too embarrassing. I don't know this girl, and she'll think I'm crazy,* that day of my life would have been far less than what God intended. He knew the blessing it would be for both of us, so He gave me an opportunity to partner with Him in reaching out to a lonely, hurting young woman.

As Christians, you and I have been called to be obedient to God in the big things and the little things. We make obedience difficult at times because we tend to focus on how difficult we think it is going to be, but we should think about how happy we will be once we have done what God wants us to do. When you make the choice to obey God no matter what, good things always happen.

2. Love in the Moment

For many people, their days are ruined because of the way someone treated them. An insult, a rumor, an unkind word from a friend or a coworker steals their joy and sends them into a downward spiral. I was like that for many years. If someone said or did something unkind toward me, I would wallow in misery for hours. *How could they? Why would they say that? Life isn't fair!*

With God's help, I've learned over the years that I am responsible for my own attitude and happiness. I cannot control what other people do, but with God's help, I can control how I respond. God has often reminded me that what someone may do to me that is unjust or unkind isn't nearly as important as how I respond to their actions.

This is where "love in the moment" comes in. When we become people who love others around us on a daily basis, our lives are tremendously enriched. Jesus said in John 15:12 (NKJV): "love one another,"

> Love is a decision we make about how we will treat all the people in our lives.

and verse 11 says that you do this so that "your joy may be full." Did you see that? Loving others actually fills your life with joy! Love is not just a feeling we have; it is a decision we make about how we will treat all the people in our lives—the ones we like and the ones that we don't like.

My husband, Dave, and I recently celebrated our fifty-year wedding anniversary. I've learned a lot about love and marriage over the years, but one of the best things I've learned is the importance of not wasting a day—loving in the moment.

When Dave comes home, telling me all about his golf game that day, I have to be honest, it doesn't always interest me. I'm not a golfer; it's just not something I enjoy. But Dave loves it! So when he is telling me about an impossible putt he made or a drive that went farther than he expected, I have a choice to make. I can selfishly think, *Dave, I'm not really interested in hearing more about golf,* and then those thoughts will show up in my attitude, or I can realize this is an opportunity to show love right in that moment. If it's important to him, I should patiently listen even if I would rather not.

Today Dave suggested to me that I come to the golf course and watch him hit golf balls at the driving range. He thought it would be a way for me to enjoy some time outside in the sun. Well, I'm more of a doer than I am a watcher, and I didn't think it would be something I would enjoy all that much, but it was the second or third time he has suggested it in the past couple of years, so I finally realized that he wanted me to observe and be proud of how well he hits the golf ball. It was a way I could love him in the moment, just as he has loved me thousands of times and sat in meetings when I was teaching.

When we do things for others that we would rather not do, we may not feel joy at the moment, but taking those moments to show love are some of the main ingredients in living a life that we can love. Doing the right thing always ultimately produces the reward of joy. After going and watching Dave hit golf balls, I was glad I did.

That's just a small example of loving in the moment. There are so many opportunities God gives each day to share love, not only with our spouse, but with friends, family, coworkers, and even complete strangers. Don't miss those chances (those moments) to show love. Your life will be so much better when you look for ways to express love to others. Remember...if love is the central theme of our life, then we will love the life we are living!

> If love is the central theme of our life, then we will love the life we are living!

3. Enjoy the Moment

So many people have the mentality that they will be really happy at some time in the future. When the kids grow up, when they get a promotion, when their finances improve...when, when, when.

I can certainly relate. There was a time, even when

I was serving the Lord in ministry, that I was always looking ahead to the time when things would be better. I wasn't enjoying the daily blessings that came my way because I was too busy looking ahead. I had to learn (and still have to remind myself) to maximize the moment and enjoy what God is doing in me and through me *now*, not when the conference is over, when the ministry is bigger, or when I can go on vacation.

I really want you to get this: God wants you to enjoy your life *now*, not at some time in the future.

Henry Ward Beecher said, "The sun does not shine for a few trees and flowers, but for the wide world's joy."[2] I love this quote. With each new sunrise, God wants all of us to live in complete and total joy. Perhaps you should stop for a moment and ask yourself if you believe that God wants you to be happy and enjoy your life. Of course He does! There are certainly many things on God's mind and heart that are important to Him, things like our obedience and spiritual growth, but He also wants us to enjoy our life!

It is amazing to me that even in the midst of running the universe, God still has us on His mind. The psalmist David said that if we tried to count God's thoughts toward us, they would be more in number than all the grains of sand that exist (see Psalm

139:17–18). Just think about it—*God has you on His mind all of the time!*

Jesus actually said that He wanted His own joy to be made full and complete in us (see John 17:13). Seeing this Scripture, and many others that are like it, settled the issue for me: *God wants us to live a life that we love and enjoy!*

Anybody can get sidetracked and focus on the problems or burdens of the day. We all have inconveniences and irritations we have to face on a regular basis. But only those who truly believe that God wants them to enjoy and love their lives will look past life's problems in order to enjoy each new day to the fullest. For some reason, we tend to think that as long as we have problems, it just wouldn't be right to not worry and instead enjoy life. But that is exactly what God wants us to do, and it is what the devil does not want us to do.

One of God's greatest gifts to us is that He enables us by His grace to enjoy life even in the midst of trouble and difficulty. The apostle Paul tells us that in the midst of all of our sufferings, we are more than conquerors through Christ Who loves us (see Romans 8:37).

Keep in mind, joy isn't based on having everything go your way all the time or laughing all day long. Joy is deeper than that. Joy can be extreme hilarity or calm delight...and everything in between! I'm a more serious person by nature, so the "calm delight" definition is usually my state of joy. But a good enthusiastic laugh is sometimes just what you need. Last night we were with our daughter and son-in-law and two of

> Joy can be extreme hilarity or calm delight... and everything in between!

our grandchildren, and something got us laughing so hard that we were actually doubled over with it. It was just something silly, but once we got started we couldn't seem to stop, and I noticed when it was finally over that I actually felt energized and as if a fresh, pleasant breeze had blown through my soul.

Philippians 4:4 says: "Rejoice in the Lord always [delight, take pleasure in Him]; again I will say, rejoice!" Notice, the Word of God doesn't just say it once—we are instructed twice to "rejoice." It's important (doubly important) to God that you rejoice each day, because He knows how powerfully it will affect your life. The joy of the Lord is our strength (see Nehemiah 8:10).

So make a decision right now to enjoy the moment. If you have a tendency to be too serious, laugh a little. Remember, God loves you always—that's something to be joyful about.

Moments, One After Another

I read recently that someone asked a woman named Nadine Stair of Louisville, Kentucky, a very poignant question. Ms. Stair, who was eighty-five years old, was asked: "What would you do differently if you had your life to live over again?" This is what Ms. Stair said:

> I'd make more mistakes next time. I'd relax.
> I would limber up. I would be sillier than I
> have been on this trip...I would climb more
> mountains and swim more rivers. I would
> eat more ice cream and less beans...I've
> had my moments, and if I had to do it over
> again, I'd have more of them. In fact, I'd
> try to have nothing else. Just moments, one
> after another, instead of living so many years
> ahead of each day...I would start barefoot
> earlier in the spring and stay that way later in
> the fall. I would go to more dances. I would
> ride more merry-go-rounds and I would pick
> more daisies.[3]

I love the attitude of this thoughtful senior citizen, because essentially what she is talking about is maximizing every moment. As she looked back over her life, she didn't wish she had worked harder or worried more; she wished she had enjoyed each day. The jokes, the weather, ice cream, spring and fall, dances, merry-go-rounds, and daisies—these are the moments she wanted to relive.

Let me ask you, "If you had to live your life over again, what would you do differently?" I doubt you'd spend more time in fear or worry, dread or regret. If you're like me, you would probably want to spend more time laughing, loving, and truly enjoying each day. Well, the good news is this: You can get started today. The missed opportunities of the past are nothing compared to the fresh opportunities of the present. With God's help, you can begin to maximize each new moment He gives you, and you don't have to wait another moment to get started.

Remember, you get 86,400 seconds today...how are you going to spend them?

Don't Forget...

- Yesterday is over; tomorrow is not promised; you can live only in the present.
- Being obedient to God is one of the best ways to live a joyful, overcoming life.

- If you'll look for opportunities to love others on a daily basis, your life will be tremendously enriched.
- Don't wait until some time in the future to begin enjoying your life. Maximize every moment you have today to love the life Jesus came to give you.

Dost thou love life? Then do not squander time, for that is the stuff life is made of.

Benjamin Franklin

CHAPTER 3

Refuse to Let Fear Determine Your Destiny

You cannot swim for new horizons until you have courage to lose sight of the shore.

William Faulkner

The morning of June 2, 2011, seemed pretty normal, like any other day for Laurie Ann Eldridge. When she woke up that sleepy morning, the thirty-nine-year-old, single mother of two teenage boys had no idea she would be faced with a life-or-death decision before the end of the day, but that was exactly what happened.

Hours later, as the evening sun began to sink into the summer horizon, Laurie was outside, working in her garden when she noticed something terrifying. A confused, elderly driver was stuck in her vehicle on a nearby railroad crossing...and Laurie could hear the whistle of an oncoming freight train. It was like a scene straight out of an action thriller, but Laurie was no actor and this was no movie.

With little time to deliberate, Laurie sprung into action.

Now before I go on, there are some things I need to tell you about this brave homemaker: Laurie had no rescue training, she was undersized at 115 pounds, she wasn't wearing any shoes, and—most important to note—Laurie suffered from a disabling back injury. She had not run a step in more than ten years.

But Laurie didn't allow any of those things to keep her from doing what she knew she needed to do.

Knowing time was of the essence, Laurie sprinted out of the garden and ran as fast as she could toward the stranded vehicle, crossing a creek and climbing an embankment in the process. When she arrived at the car, she shouted for eighty-one-year-old Angeline Pascucci to exit the vehicle. Realizing Ms. Pascucci was too confused to act on her own, Laurie reached into the car, unlocked the door, and pulled the elderly woman from the car. "All I could think about was the lady's face. She looked lost. She needed help, and she needed help right then," Laurie would later tell reporters.

With the forty-seven-car freight train bearing down mercilessly upon them, Laurie, her feet bloody and riddled with splinters, tumbled down the embankment with Angeline Pascucci in her arms, just seconds before the train demolished the automobile.

Laurie Ann Eldridge would later be recognized with a medal from the Carnegie Hero Fund Commission, which honors civilians who exhibit lifesaving acts of bravery. Her courage saved a life that day and gave us all an inspirational example of courage in the face of fear.[4]

Courage to Move Forward

There are so many things about Laurie's story that I love, but one thing in particular stands out: Laurie didn't allow *anything* to slow her down. It didn't matter that she was undersized (smaller even than the woman she rescued); she didn't hesitate even though she had no shoes on; and she leapt into action in spite of a back injury that had limited her for the last decade. *Nothing* was going to keep her from taking action.

I include that story in this chapter because there are far too many people who have allowed fear to slow them down or completely stop them from doing what they truly want to do. Being afraid we will fail, afraid of what others might say, afraid the past will repeat itself, afraid we don't have what it takes to succeed—these fears (and so many others) often keep us from living the abundant, overcoming life God has planned for us to live.

If you want to truly love your life, there may be some things you will need to change, and if you let fear stop you, it will keep you trapped where you are. For example, many people hate their jobs; if that is the case, the only way to fix it is to either get a new attitude or a new job! If that is you, I urge you to take action and refuse to spend your life doing something you hate just because the pay is good, or because it's what you have always done and you're afraid of change. If we do not live courageously, we will have no hope of loving our lives, and we probably won't even like them.

Everyone deals with fear at some time in their lives. That's why it is so important for us to understand what fear is and how we can push through it whenever it arises. You can't love your life until you decide to be a strong, confi-

> You can't love your life until you decide to be a strong, confident, courageous person!

dent, courageous person! If we do not confront and move past fear, we will find that we often look back in regret as we ponder all the things that we wish we would have done and did not even try to do because of fear.

Fear usually begins as a thought—an anxious thought, a hesitant thought. *Maybe I can't do this. I'm going to get hurt if I try. People will laugh at me.* Those thoughts can become strong, intense feelings that keep us from doing something that would be beneficial for our lives. Fear is one of Satan's most effective tools to manipulate people and keep them out of God's will. Recently, I was visited with the spirit of fear as I pondered doing something courageous. It presented itself as a sinking feeling in my soul. I recall thinking about how much I disliked that feeling. I remember being glad that I knew enough about how the devil operates that I was able to resist him, but there were a lot of years in my life when I didn't know to resist, and fear controlled many of my decisions. We are not created by God to shrink back in fear, but to boldly go forward as we trust Him to never leave us or forsake us.

The best way to understand it is this: Fear is the opposite of faith. God wants us to live in faith, trusting His plan for our lives, but the enemy wants us to shrink back in fear. It is only when we learn to live by faith, moving forward regardless of the worry or anxiety we may *feel*, that we can live a fulfilling, satisfying, contented, and joyful life in Christ.

You may think, *Well, how do I do that? How do I find the strength to choose faith over fear? After all, there are a lot of scary things out there to deal with. How do I move forward even when I am afraid?* I think those are very good questions, and I've discovered the answer may be easier than you think.

Focusing on God's promises instead of the world's problems is the best way to overcome fear. Just as we must feed our bodies with food to keep them healthy and strong, we must feed our faith with God's promises in order for it to stay strong.

> Focusing on God's promises is the best way to overcome fear.

- Instead of obsessing over an economic downturn, choose to remember that God promises to meet all your needs (see Philippians 4:19).
- Rather than focus on what seems impossible, dwell on the fact that all things are possible with God on your side (see Matthew 19:26).
- When the doctor's report is discouraging, focus on the assurance of healing in God's Word (see Isaiah 53:5).
- If you feel alone and on your own, never forget that God is always with you (see Deuteronomy 31:6).

Quite often I experience doubt trying to crowd its way into my heart, and I begin to falter in my faith. But if I go to my Bible and read God's promises, or if I meditate on them, I can feel the doubt being pushed aside and my faith getting strong once again. It's the promises in God's Word that give you the strength to stand when everyone else around seems to be falling. When you focus on the Word of God and the promises for your life that God has given you, worry, anxiety, and fear lose their strength and you once again find yourself enjoying and loving your life.

What Are You Afraid Of?

One of the best things you can do is take a personal inventory, asking yourself: *What am I afraid of? Are there any areas in my life where progress is being hindered because of fear?* When you can identify your fears, you can deal with them head-on. Remember, it's not wrong to feel afraid (in fact, it's quite natural), but you don't have to let the fear control your decisions and actions. You can push through it, knowing that fear is just a weapon of the enemy trying to keep you from God's best.

David said, "When I am afraid, I will put my trust and faith in You" (Psalm 56:3). Notice that David didn't deny he was afraid. But when he felt fear, he trusted God and kept going. He didn't let it slow him down. I can confidently say that when God leads you to step out in an area and do something new, or when He leads you to make a bigger commitment, you will probably feel fear. But if you are sure God is leading you, then put your confidence in Him and boldly move forward. Even if we take only one small step at a time, we will eventually arrive at our desired destination as long as we refuse to give up.

I remember a time when we knew we needed more office space to handle the growth of the ministry. We needed computers, desks, more employees, and so on. I had prayed for growth so we could help more people with the truth of God's Word, but it was intimidating to think about the cost and energy required to move forward.

I had a choice to make: We could make the necessary moves and step forward in faith, or we could shrink back and freeze in fear. It would have been very easy to let the uncertainty and potential problems hold us back. And I was certainly tempted to give in to fear. I had thoughts like, *Joyce, maybe you're going too fast. This could be a complete failure. Are you sure this is a good idea?*

I'm sure you've had thoughts like that in areas of your life, too. When you felt led to start a new career, *What if I fall on my face?* As you were raising your children, *Maybe I'm doing it all wrong.* When you reached out to help someone, *What if they tell me to mind my own business?* But if you'll stand

> If you'll stand on the promises of God's Word and move forward in faith, you'll be amazed at the joy that comes with moving past your fears.

on the promises of God's Word and move forward in faith, you'll be amazed at the joy that comes with moving past your fears.

In my situation, God met our every need. It wasn't always easy, and there were certainly days when our faith was tested. We found ourselves wondering if we had made the right decisions, but as we pushed past the fear and trusted God, He always provided. It didn't always happen in the ways we expected or in the timing we would have chosen, but He did meet our needs, and His way was better than we could have even imagined. I look back now and I am so thankful that I didn't let fear stop me. That is one of the reasons I am so strongly encouraging you not to let it slow you down or stop you, either. If you don't follow your heart and do the things you truly want to do and believe you are supposed to do, then you will live in regret—and that will definitely prevent you from loving your life.

So as you search your heart, identifying areas of fear today, take it one step further: Search God's Word and find what He has to say about those fears. Don't let the problems slow you down any longer; instead, let the promises of God be an accelerating force in your life. Here are a few of those accelerating promises you can depend on right now:

Do not fear [anything], for I am with you; do not be afraid, for I am your God. I will strengthen you, be assured I will help you; I will certainly take hold of you with My righteous right hand [a hand of justice, of power, of victory, of salvation].

Isaiah 41:10

For God did not give us a spirit of timidity or cowardice or fear, but [He has given us a spirit] of power and of love and of sound judgment and personal discipline [abilities that result in a calm, well-balanced mind and self-control].

2 Timothy 1:7

There is no fear in love [dread does not exist]. But perfect (complete, full-grown) love drives out fear.

1 John 4:18

Don't Let Anything Hold You Back

Laurie Ann Eldridge was brave, even though she had no rescue experience. She was determined, even with no shoes on her feet. She ran, even though she hadn't run in ten years. What about you? Will you reject the limitations in your life and run toward the opportunities in front of you?

I understand if you're afraid, and I know there are legitimate challenges you might face, but just think about the reward involved. If you'll say no to fear and yes to God, there is a life ahead of you full of potential, wonder, and new possibilities. Don't let fear slow you down any longer. Run into your future and watch God do something incredible with your life!

Don't Forget…

- It is only when we learn to live by faith, moving forward regardless of the fear we may *feel*, that we can live a fulfilling, satisfying, and joyful life in Christ.
- Focusing on God's promises instead of your problems is the best way to overcome fear.
- If you believe God is leading you in a certain direction, put your confidence in Him and take a step of faith.
- You'll never regret moving forward in obedience to God's leading in your life.

There is only one
happiness in this life, to
love and be loved.

George Sand

CHAPTER 4

The Power of Grace

May the perfect grace and eternal love of Christ our Lord be our never-failing protection and help.

Saint Ignatius

Have you ever thought about what powers your life?

Consider a car, a boat, a stove, or even something simple like a hair dryer. All of these things are powered by *something*—gasoline, electricity, solar energy, or natural gas. Without a sustaining power source, they won't function properly.

Now what about you? What is the power source for your life? If the answer is something that is dependent on you, such as your intellect, your sense of independence, your strong work ethic, your education, or your winning personality, I must warn you that your life isn't going to function properly. It might sputter on for a little while, but eventually you'll discover that none of those power sources are enough to sustain you and enable you to enjoy life.

And if the source that powers your life is built around another person such as your spouse, your children, the satisfaction you get from your job, your friendships, or even your church life, the outcome won't be much better. Sadly, people can let us down. Relationships are important, but they mustn't be the thing we depend on to fuel our lives. Other people can be great blessings to our lives, but they will always fall short of being our sole source of power.

Let me tell you about the amazing gift God has given us that serves as the fuel (the power) for our lives—His grace.

Grace Really Is Amazing

I've discovered that all of us—even people who have been Christians for a long time—have struggles from time to time. None of us are immune to frustrating habits, disappointing failures, or occasionally feeling like we just can't make it. But the good news is this: Once you get a revelation of God's grace in your life, you find the power to overcome those struggles.

Let me show you what I mean...

Think about a problem you may be dealing with in your life right now—a bad habit, a frustration at work, a conflict in a relationship, or anything similar that is weighing on your mind. Now, I want to ask you: Have you been *trying* in your own strength to make things work out? If so, how has that worked for you? Have you solved your problem, or have you come up short of the perfect solution?

If you're still dealing with the same frustration, don't get discouraged—you are in the best place to realize just how amazing God's grace really is! You see, grace is God's power, not ours. Grace is the power to overcome bad habits, to make peace in a relationship, or to bring you victoriously through any trial without all of your *trying* in your own strength. Simply put, grace is the power of God that enables us to do with ease what we could never do on our own.

The only thing that our trying, or self-effort, ever does is cause frustration, because we are trying in our own strength. We can never make ourselves better without God's help. It is interesting to note that *trying* is not a biblical principle. Yes, the word "trying" is in the Bible, but it's not there telling us to try to do better or be better. When you study the Word, you see that "trying" is used in reference to the "trying of our faith," "trying of the spirits," or "trying us to prove our character." All of our *trying*, or human

> *Grace is the power of God that enables us to do with ease what we could never do on our own.*

effort apart from God, is really just works of the flesh, and it will never bring about lasting change. Only God's power—His grace—can do that.

Don't get me wrong: It is great to want to be a better person, and the Bible does instruct us to make every effort to live godly lives (see 2 Peter 1:5). There is certainly nothing bad about that. In fact, it's a desire God gives us, but Galatians 3:10 tells us very clearly that "anyone who tries to live by his own effort, independent of God, is doomed to failure" (MSG). That is why we often find ourselves frustrated or overwhelmed by different situations in our lives— we're trying to work it out on our own, and that will never do. If you've found yourself in that situation, the solution is simple. All you have to do is...

Ask God for His Help

God loves you more than you could ever imagine. If you have accepted Jesus as your Savior, you are God's child, and it gives Him joy to help you. But He will never force His help on you at any time. You have the choice to try to do things in your own strength or to ask for His help and guidance in your life. Far too many times, we stubbornly try to fix our-selves and work out situations in our own strength. I really believe it breaks God's heart when He sees us struggling with situations in life when all we need to do is stop and ask Him for help.

God taught me this truth in a way I'll never forget...

My husband, Dave, is pretty tall, but I am not. We have a really high window over the kitchen sink in our house. When that window is open, there's no way for me to close it without a lot of effort and a big ordeal. Now, how do you think Dave would feel if every time I needed that window closed, I ran out of the house to go ask the man next door to come help me? Or what if I tried to do it by myself, straining and stretching, maybe climbing up on the counter, possibly knocking things over, getting all worn-out...while Dave was sitting right there? The truth is, that would really be insulting to him. It would definitely hurt Dave if I refused to rely on his help when I needed it.

In the same way, it grieves God to watch us struggle so needlessly, when all the while, He is right there waiting for us to simply exchange *trying* for *trusting*. Whatever you may be going through today, all you have to do is trust God and ask for His help— His grace. That grace provides the power for you to live an abundant life. Striving, struggling, and trying can never do that. Ephesians 2:8–9 tells us very clearly:

It is by grace you have been saved, through faith—and this is not from yourselves, it is *the gift of God—not by works, so that no one can boast* (NIV). (Emphasis added.)

In the same way that you are saved by God's grace, you can live each day of your life in the power of God's grace. It's the best way to live! All you have to do is humble yourself, ask God for His help, and then do what

> All you have to do is trust God and ask for His help.

He tells you to do. You can trust Him, rather than your own self-effort, because He is mighty and can do whatever you need Him to do. You'll have a part to play, but God will give you the strength to do whatever He asks you to do. Trust in His goodness—He loves you so much, and He wants to help you no matter what you are going through. Isn't that amazing?

Keep in mind that God has called us to enter His rest. He does not want us to be frustrated, but instead He desires that we enjoy peace. Jesus said that He left us His peace, but that we need to stop allowing ourselves to be upset and disturbed, fearful and intimidated (see John 14:27 AMPC). I have learned that when I feel frustrated, it means that I have allowed myself to enter into works of the flesh, which is me trying to do in my own strength what only God can do, and that I need to renew my commitment to receive God's grace and work with Him instead of trying to work without Him.

Frustration is a calling card that reminds me to once again lean and rely on God instead of on myself or other people, and it can be the same thing for you.

Grace to Love Your Life

I believe there is grace available to us every day of our lives for every situation we face. God is not surprised or caught off guard when we encounter a challenging situation. He knew what you were going to have to deal with long before you did, and He has already provided everything you need to learn from it and come out of it better off than before. This is why the Bible says we can "rejoice in the Lord *always*" (Philippians 4:4; emphasis added). God is never going to put us in a situation or permit us to be in a circumstance without giving us the ability to be there with joy.

The power of grace is so essential to living a life you love, because God's power on your behalf does more than help you just survive life—grace gives you the ability to live an overcoming, confident, joy-filled life in Christ. Hard things can be done with ease when we do them by God's grace.

I've heard people say things like, "I'm staying in this situation," or "I am trying to do this because I believe it's what God wants me to do, but I am so incredibly miserable and unhappy." Well, I'm convinced this is not how God works. It may not always be easy, but if God has placed you in a situation, He is going to give you a special

> Hard things can be done with ease when we do them by God's grace.

grace to be there. I like this statement: *"God gives us grace for our place."* That means you will have peace and joy in the midst of what you're encountering. People may wonder how you can do what you are doing and remain so peaceful, and it is a great testimony of God's power at work in your life.

Let me give you an example. For many people, public speaking is a frightening endeavor. They get nervous just thinking about getting up and talking in front of a crowd, much less actually doing it. But I love to stand up in front of large groups of people and teach the Word of God. I speak in front of thousands of people at our conferences and crusades without any problem at all. And there is only one reason I can do this—it's the grace of God. God has given me grace (His power) in that area to do what He has called me to do. People say to me all the time, "Joyce, I don't know how you do it!" But it is not difficult for me, because God has given me grace for my place. This grace enables me to love and enjoy my life.

In the same way, there are things you do—parts of your life—that other people probably wouldn't have the patience, ability, or energy to do. Whether it's raising small children, working a particular job, functioning in a certain ministry role, or dealing with a unique challenge, God has given you a grace to do it because that's part of His plan for your life. You receive His grace (undeserved favor and power) by faith, and you need to remember that when these areas of life get difficult (and they certainly will), don't step out of God's grace. Don't try to persevere on your own or find the solution in your own strength. Instead, rely on God, trusting that He will give you the instruction and answers you need to keep going. You may have to do it one day at a time or even one moment at a time, but I think you'll find that when you keep your focus and your dependence on God, your level of joy will be much higher.

I want you to remember that works of the flesh equals frustration, but grace enables us to do with ease what we could never do on our own with any amount of struggle and effort.

There Is a Way

The attitude we live with—the level of joy, the level of peace, the level of stability we have—is what determines how much or how little we enjoy each and every day of our lives. If you've been in this world very long at all, you've learned that there are very few days that go exactly the way you'd like them to. Just today as I am writing this book, we have severe flood warnings in our city. We are facing the challenge and inconvenience of being shut-in for a few days, because all the highways and roads that lead to our home will be closed. I have several appointments that will need to be rearranged, and I need to leave town for a conference. If that isn't enough, I just walked through my house and heard a drip, drip, drip, and after investigating, discovered that my ceiling is leaking water onto the floor and fireplace mantel.

I can get upset and distracted from what I am doing, or I can do what I'm able to do and trust God to take care of all the things that I cannot do. Until we stop letting our joy be determined by our circumstances, we will never enjoy stability. The psalmist David said that when we dwell in the presence of the Most High, we will "remain stable and fixed under the shadow of the Almighty [Whose power no foe can withstand]" (Psalm 91:1 AMPC).

But in the midst of all the challenges and surprises of life, there is good news: We have a way to be happy when circumstances don't necessarily suit us, or when we don't get a breakthrough as quickly as we'd like, or when people around us are not what we'd like them to be, or when we are disappointed. And that way is the grace of God!

Remember, grace is never in short supply. You can have as much of it as you need, as often as you need it. His grace is made perfect in our weaknesses. All that we need to do is ask and receive that our joy may be full (see John 16:24). Grace is like electricity that is always coming into our homes: We don't benefit from it unless we plug something into it. Plain and simple, grace is power, and we receive that power through plugging in by faith. Perhaps you are struggling in your life because you are *unplugged*! But you can plug in right now and start to receive a flow of power immediately that will make life enjoyable.

The Bible says that every man is given a measure of faith (see Romans 12:3). The measure we are given is the exact measure we need for what God gives us to do. So instead of trying to solve our problems, fix things, or work things out on our own, we can release our faith by trusting God to take care of them. Then God's grace—His power—comes through that channel of faith and enables us to do what we couldn't do by ourselves, which will amaze others and us.

I suggest that you take a moment and offer to God anything and everything that frustrates or burdens you, naming them one by one. Release them to God and ask Him for His grace. Now take some time and receive it by faith. You may not feel that anything is different, but believe that you have received what you have asked for and then go on with your life. After you do this, if you continue to feel frustrated and miserable in the days and months ahead, then perhaps you should revisit whether or not you are doing what God wants you to do. Jesus did not die for us so we could struggle through life and merely endure it. He wants us to live fully and love completely the life He has given us.

There are times in all of our lives when we may think we are doing what we should be doing, yet nothing seems to be working right and we have lost our joy. Then we discover that God wants us to make a turn and go in another direction. It may only be a slight turn or it could be a complete U-turn, but always remember that God never calls us to do something that requires constant struggle and creates a loss of joy. Don't be afraid of change, and don't be afraid to discover that somewhere along the road of life you made a wrong turn.

Here is an example that might help. Over the years we have changed our conference schedule five times. At one time, we did 36 conferences a year, and that got to be a struggle. So we changed to 24 a year, and after several years that became a struggle, so we changed to 18 conferences a year. Then we changed to 13, and recently we made a change to 12, but we also dropped one session and are doing three instead of the four we have always done. Why did we change? Each time prior to making a change, we found that what was once easy was becoming very difficult and was draining our joy, and we knew that wasn't God's will for us.

God always gives us sufficient grace to do what He wants us to do, and the presence or absence of that grace is one of the ways we can discern whether or not we are in the will of God. We may be in the will of God doing a certain thing in one season of our life, but that thing must be laid down in order for us to go into the next season. Very few of us rarely do anything the exact same way our entire lives, and being able to sense godly seasons of change is very important to walking in the will of God.

Don't Forget…

- What are you relying on to be the power source of your life? Is it your own strength or abilities?

Is it another person or relationship? Or is it God and His grace in your life?

- Grace is God's power—not ours. Grace is the power to overcome bad habits, to make peace in a relationship, or to bring you victoriously through any trial without continual frustration and misery.

- It breaks God's heart when He sees us struggling with situations in life when all we need to do is stop and ask Him for help.

- If God has placed you in a situation, He will give you a special grace to be there. He will give you grace for your place!

- God's power comes to you freely as you put your faith in Him.

There are only two ways to live your life. One is as though nothing is a miracle. The other is as though everything is.

Albert Einstein

CHAPTER 5

Don't Poison the Present with the Past

I like the dreams of the future better than the history of the past.

Thomas Jefferson

Junk food. Air pollution. Rumors. Black mold. Dark thoughts. What do all of these things have in common? Answer: They're bad for us. Toxic. Destructive. We all know to avoid these harmful poisons. Too much access to them can destroy our bodies, our souls, or our spirits. That's common sense. We know to avoid them because they can hurt us...sometimes in irreparable ways.

Well, there is something just as destructive that lurks right around the corner of your mind. Something that is as toxic to your soul as pollution is to your body: the poison of the past. It's a danger that can limit your present happiness and destroy your future hope. The contamination of past pain or previous regret is a venom that too many are unknowingly ingesting on a daily basis.

I know this firsthand. You see, for years, my past pain dictated how I approached my life and relationships with other people. I had a hard time trusting anyone or believing I was safe around people. My relationships and my mind-set were affected by the tragic past I had endured. It was hard for me to believe that I could ever have a truly good life because I had endured a truly painful past. Until I found healing from the Lord, this was just the way I thought I was going to be: second-rate, inferior, angry, bitter, disappointed, and afraid.

But the good news is that with God's help, I learned my past didn't have to define my future. I didn't get a good start in life, but I am determined to have a good finish! I was not called by God to be a victim my whole life, and neither were you.

> I was not called by God to be a victim my whole life, and neither were you.

He has something so much better in store. When I learned that my past did not have to define me, I was able to start letting God's Word define me. It was an eye-opening discovery. I began to see that I was not a victim or a sad story—I was a child of God. I was loved, accepted, and cared for, and I had an unbelievably good future in Christ.

The same is true for you. No matter what you did in the past, or what someone did to you, you are more than your past pain. You belong to God and He has a good plan for you. Jeremiah 29:11 says:

> "For I know the plans and thoughts that I have for you," says the Lord, "plans for peace and well-being and not for disaster to give you a future and a hope."

But in order to experience that bright future, and in order to love your present life, it is vitally important that you let go of the poison of the past. When you do, you will begin to enjoy the present regardless of the past.

Healing from Past Pain

I'm encouraged when I study the Word of God to see that all throughout His ministry, Jesus brought healing—physical, mental, emotional, and spiritual healing.

- When the blind man called to Him from the side of the road, Jesus stopped and opened his eyes (see Luke 18:35–42).
- When Peter was devastated by his failure, Jesus made a point to let Peter know he still had a future (see John 21:15–21).

- When a woman caught in adultery was brought to Jesus, He offered grace and then said, "Go and sin no more" (see John 8:3–11).

These are just a few of the many examples of divine healing; Jesus never missed an opportunity to heal hurting people of their pain. And this isn't just a phenomenon limited to biblical times. Hebrews 13:8 gives us an amazing promise:

> Jesus Christ is [eternally changeless, always] the same yesterday and today and forever.

Just as Jesus healed people of their pain in the New Testament, He still heals today. Whatever pain,

> There is no pit so deep that Jesus cannot reach in and lift you out!

abuse, or disappointments you've faced in the past, Jesus can heal you so you can move forward and live a healthy, whole life in Him. There is no trauma too big or no mistake too costly— Jesus can heal it all. There is no pit so deep that Jesus cannot reach in and lift you out!

In order to keep the past from poisoning your present, this is important to know. If you want to really love your life, you must first receive the healing that is yours in Christ Jesus. If there is something from your past that is trying to poison your present (and your future), I want to encourage you to pray this prayer (or one like it) right now:

> Father, You know the pain I've endured. You know what I did, or what was done to me, in my past. You know how it has affected me and how I've been stuck in that past trauma. I pray today that You heal my soul and give me hope for a better future. I choose to let go of the past and trust You as I move forward in life. I no longer want to be held back by my past. Heal me totally and completely, and help me take the steps I need to take in order to start a brand-new life in You.

I encourage you to remember that our walk with God is a journey and our path gets brighter and brighter as we continue with Him. Don't make the mistake that so many people make, thinking that all healing should be instantaneous. Healing takes time, and we should enjoy each step and every tiny bit of progress!

New Hope for the Future

Martha Washington said, "The greater part of our happiness or misery depends upon our dispositions, and not upon our circumstances."[5] In other words, the mind-set you have regarding your future, not your current circumstances, goes a long way in determining what kind of life you are going to live.

I love how the apostle Paul says it in Ephesians 4:22–23 (AMPC). He writes:

> Strip yourselves of your former nature…and be constantly renewed in the spirit of your mind [having a fresh mental and spiritual attitude].

Having a "fresh mental and spiritual attitude" is essential if you want to discover how to love your life. You can overcome any difficult situation or pain from your past if you will just agree with God and say, "Yes, this happened in my life, but God is on my side, and I know He has a good plan for me."

With God's help, you can overcome your past and learn to have a great hope for the future. God is concerned about everything that concerns you, and don't ever think that He is too busy to help you. What

> What we may see as a dead end, God sees as a new beginning!

we may see as a dead end, God sees as a new beginning!

The Israelites couldn't see God's vision for their lives. This is why they wandered in the wilderness for forty years. They looked at everything through the prism of their past. As a matter of fact, they had so little vision for the future that they wanted to go back to Egypt and return to the life of slavery they once knew. The past wasn't good, but it was familiar to them. They kept looking back to Egypt, but all the while God wanted them to have hope for the future.

We would be wise to learn a lesson from the Israelites. If we want to see change happen in our lives, we need to get a vision that goes beyond what we've already experienced. We need to look ahead with hope for the future.The best way to do

> We need to get a vision that goes beyond what we've already experienced.

that is to stand on the promises in God's Word. For example, the Word of God says:

> I am convinced and confident of this very thing, that He who has begun a good work in you will [continue to] perfect and complete it until the day of Jesus Christ [the time of His return].
>
> Philippians 1:6

In due time and at the appointed season we shall reap, if we do not loosen and relax our courage and faint.

Galatians 6:9 (AMPC)

But the path of the [uncompromisingly] just and righteous is like the light of dawn, that shines more and more (brighter and clearer).

Proverbs 4:18 (AMPC)

These promises, and so many more just like them, give us hope that God has great things in store. You may have struggled in the past, but that doesn't mean you will always struggle. Expect something good to happen to you at any moment!

Our hope is not limited by what we can see around us or what we went through previously. Hope that sustains us is hope that is based on the Word of God and His promises for our lives. God is always doing something new. This is why Isaiah 43:18–19 says: "Forget the former things; do not dwell on the past. See, I am doing a new thing! Now it springs up; do you not perceive it? I am making a way in the wilderness and streams in the wasteland" (NIV).

> Hope that sustains us is hope that is based on the Word of God and His promises for our lives.

If your past could easily be described as a "wilderness" or a "wasteland," take hope—God is doing a new thing! Simply follow His plan rather than your own thoughts or feelings (those are unreliable). Look past your circumstances and focus on the promises God has laid out for you in His Word. This will give you the hope you need to begin loving your life.

Satan does not want you to enjoy or love your life, and he will do all that he can to discourage you and try to make you think that nothing good will ever happen to you. He is a liar, and the truth is not in him, so don't listen to him. Jesus said,

> The thief comes only in order to steal and kill and destroy. I came that they may have and enjoy life, and have it in abundance [to the full, till it overflows].
>
> John 10:10

Vision to See Past Your Circumstances

When it comes to getting a vision for the future, some people get confused. "What does that mean? How do I have a vision? Is that just spiritual lingo?" Well, let me show you an example of what I'm talking about.

In Genesis 13, Abraham had a big choice to make. You see, he and his nephew, Lot, had too much cattle to feed on the land. It was just too crowded, and the limited space was causing problems. So Abraham said to Lot, "Let's go our separate ways. I'll let you choose what land you want. I'll give you first pick." Selfishly, Lot chose the best part of the Jordan valley for himself.

This was where Abraham's choice came into play. Abraham could have gotten angry and had a bad attitude. He could have insisted, "That's not fair! How could you?" But instead, Abraham trusted that God had a good future for him. He trusted God's goodness, knowing that God was in control.

In verses 14–15, this is what happened: "The LORD said to Abram after Lot had parted from him, 'Look around from where you are, to the north and south, to the east and west. All the land that you see I will give to you and your offspring forever'" (NIV).

This is an example of vision! Rather than focus on his circumstances (Lot taking what appeared to be the best land), Abraham trusted God's best for his future...and it paid off. The Lord showed him all the good things that were in store. Well, in much the same way, God has shown you all the good things in store for your life. That's what the promises in His Word are all about. If you'll look past your circumstances, trust God, and stand on His promises, He'll give you the vision to see that He will bless you in ways greater than you can imagine. God's promises are for anyone who will believe them. What we believe is our choice, so why not believe something good?

So let me encourage you: Stop thinking about everything you've lost, everything you think you're not, the way you've been treated in the past, and everything you feel like you've given up. Instead, set your mind on God's vision for your future. God's Word tells us that when the thief is discovered, he must restore seven times what he has stolen (see Proverbs 6:31). When we stop blaming God, other people, and our circumstances for our unhappy lives and put the blame where it rightfully belongs, which is on the devil, our healing can begin.

Focus on God's healing for your life and His great plan for moving you forward. When you do, you'll find that the pain of yesterday will begin to fade away and new hope for tomorrow will grow brighter and brighter. Meditate on these promises, and as you do so, they will feed your faith and keep it strong.

> Return to the stronghold [of security and prosperity], O prisoners who have the hope; even today I am declaring that I will restore double [your former prosperity] to you.
> Zechariah 9:12

The Lord restored the fortunes of Job when he prayed for his friends, and the Lord gave Job twice as much as he had before.

Job 42:10

The Lord will cause the enemies who rise up against you to be defeated before you; they will come out against you one way, but flee before you seven ways.

Deuteronomy 28:7

Instead of your [former] shame you shall have a twofold recompense; instead of dishonor and reproach [your people] shall rejoice in their portion. Therefore in their land they shall possess double [what they had forfeited]; everlasting joy shall be theirs.

Isaiah 61:7 (AMPC)

Antidotes and Life-Giving Nutrients

We began this chapter talking about the things that can poison our lives—most notably, the poison of the past. God's Word contains the answer to every problem we could ever encounter, and it gives life to those who believe it. The Bible is filled with antidotes for those poisons, for example...

- God loves you unconditionally and He always will.
- Understand that all your sins have been forgiven. When you ask God for His forgiveness, He remembers your faults no more!
- Follow the guidance and instruction of the Holy Spirit. Simply ask God for His peace and wisdom, and He will show you the steps to take!
- Live in the joy of knowing that you are not alone. God is with you, and He promises to never leave your side!
- Trust that God is your protection. No matter who or what stands against you, God is your defender. Let Him fight your battles...He never loses!
- Embrace the Bible-based hope that great things are in store for your future!

If you'll hold on to these good things from your Heavenly Father, there is no way the past can hold you back any longer. You will never again live as a victim of previous pain or circumstances. Instead, you'll thrive in the life God has for you.

Fight the good fight of faith and don't let the enemy steal, kill, or destroy another day of your life. The past is over, the present is here, and God's future lies ahead of you. He has a life full of hope, purpose, strength, and promise in store. That's a life you can truly love!

Don't Forget...

- With God's help, your past doesn't have to define your future.
- Jesus is the great healer. He can heal you of any past pain or trauma. Simply ask for His healing and trust that He will do it.
- Having a "fresh mental and spiritual attitude" is essential if you want to discover how to love your life.
- You are a dear child of God with an incredible future promised to you.
- If you'll look past your circumstances, trust God, and stand on His promises, He'll bless you in ways greater than you can imagine.

A great book begins with an idea; a great life, with a determination.

Louis L'Amour

CHAPTER 6

Count Your Blessings

Reflect upon your present blessings—of which every man has many—not your past misfortunes, of which all men have some.

Charles Dickens

I recently heard about a conversation R. C. Chapman, a renowned pastor and evangelist, had with a friend, and this exchange touched me in a profound way. The story goes that Chapman was asked one morning how he was feeling. It's a simple question, one we've all been asked a thousand times—"How are you doing today?"

Chapman's response stuck with me. He said, "I'm burdened this morning." His friend was a little confused, because Chapman said those words with a huge smile on his face. The questioner inquired, "Are you really burdened, Mr. Chapman?"

"Yes, but it's a wonderful burden. It's an overabundance of blessings for which I cannot find enough time or words to express my gratitude," R. C. Chapman replied. Seeing that his friend was still puzzled,

Chapman went on to say, "I am referring to Psalm 68:19, which fully describes my condition. In that verse, the Father in Heaven reminds us that He 'daily loads us with benefits.'"

Wow! I love that attitude, and I love that verse of Scripture. Psalm 68:19 in full says: "Blessed be the Lord, who daily loadeth us with benefits, even the God of our salvation" (KJV).

R. C. Chapman was trying to tell his friend something we would all be wise to understand: "God has blessed me so much that I can hardly stand it! I'm loaded down with blessings!" This attitude, this outlook on life, is an important step in learning to love the life God has given you.

Now, you may read those words from Mr. Chapman and think, *I don't feel that blessed. I mean, I recognize I have some blessings in my life, but I'm certainly not overwhelmed by blessings.* Well, that's why I've included this chapter in this book—I want to remind you how truly blessed you are!

You see, it's easy to overlook the good things God has given us. We can often get busy with the tasks and challenges of our daily lives. So busy, in fact, that we easily overlook the countless blessings we enjoy. But this is why so many people are living frustrated, joyless, disappointing lives. They've simply forgotten—or maybe they never even realized—how blessed they really are.

A couple of years ago, I made a decision in January. I set a goal for myself to be thankful for at least one blessing every day of the year. All year long, I tried my best to do that, and in the process I learned something valuable: Complaining didn't change anything. Focusing on a negative problem or situation didn't make the situation any better—all it did was make me feel worse. But when I chose to look for and focus on the good things, I began to enjoy every day in a way I never had before.

Through the years, I have made many lists to remind myself of God's goodness and His blessings. And to this very day, I can look at those lists and be encouraged. A few of the things I've written on these lists are:

- The love of my family and friends
- The privilege of teaching God's Word
- Being able to reach out and help people
- God's daily provisions
- Clean water and good food

These are just a few examples of God's blessings. Each time I look at these things, I feel content and peaceful all over again. By counting my blessings, my entire outlook and attitude about life improve tremendously...and yours will, too.

Back to the Basics

James 1:17 says: "Every good thing given and every perfect gift is from above; it comes down from the Father." I share that verse with you because I am convinced it is a spiritually foundational principle we need to remember. *Every* good thing we have has been given to us by God to help us enjoy our lives.

One of the very first things we teach our children is how to count. It's so cute to watch their little faces light up when we praise them for remembering that four comes after three, and ten is the number of fingers they have. We happily exclaim, "You are so smart! What a great counter you are!"

I still remember how my kids (and now my grandkids) would come home from preschool and kindergarten showing off how high they were learning to count. "Mommy, I can count to fifty! Grandma, listen to me count to a hundred!" It's one of the first things they learned...and they were so happy and eager to demonstrate their newfound skills.

I'm sure you can relate. Surely, you've watched a son or daughter, a niece or nephew, proudly count on their fingers or confidently show you their basic math skills. Counting is a rite of passage. It's the foundation for every math problem we'll ever solve.

Well, just like the skill of basic counting is

foundational for our children, I believe the skill of counting our blessings is foundational for every Christian. When we learn to focus on the good things God has done for us, rather than the

> *The skill of counting our blessings is foundational for every Christian.*

trouble or distractions we may be facing, there is absolutely nothing that can steal our joy! Although this is something that most of us know we should do, we often forget it and need to be reminded.

I think about the way I used to live my life and it is no wonder I was upset, discouraged, and frustrated all the time. You see, I was a person who would focus on the negative events and happenings of my day. I can't tell you how many of my days were ruined because of something someone said or something that didn't go the way I had planned for it to go.

It wasn't because I was a bad person. In fact, I was trying to be the best person I could. I loved God, and I was passionate about studying His Word. However, I didn't yet understand the foundational benefits of counting my blessings. Instead of seeing the good things in my life, I was focusing on the negative things. Rather than counting my blessings, I was actually doing the opposite—I was counting my disappointments. It went something like this:

What has gone wrong today? Well, hmm, let's see...

#1: Dave went golfing instead of spending time with me.

#2: A friend canceled our coffee date.

#3: The grocery store was out of what I needed.

#4: The kids are really frustrating me.

Do you get the picture? It is no wonder I was unhappy. I was putting my energy into counting the wrong things!

Have you ever found yourself obsessing about all the things that went wrong today rather than all the things that were right? Have you ever spent the evening telling your spouse or your friend about every bad thing about your day instead of every good thing? If you have, don't get too down on yourself. I think we have all fallen into the negativity trap. Bad news is like bad headlines—it gets all the attention.

But rather than focus on the negative events of your day, let me encourage you to get back to the spiritual basics and take a refresher course in counting your blessings. Here are a few ways to do that:

- *Remember* the Word of God instructs us to "not forget" God's blessings.

> Bless and affectionately praise the Lord, O
> my soul, and do not forget any of His benefits.
>
> Psalm 103:2

- *Realize* that God has blessed us with "every spiritual blessing."

> Blessed and worthy of praise be the God
> and Father of our Lord Jesus Christ, who
> has blessed us with every spiritual blessing
> in the heavenly realms in Christ.
>
> Ephesians 1:3

- *Rejoice* that even when you're having a bad day, God is there to carry you through it.

> Blessed be the Lord, Who bears our burdens
> and carries us day by day, even the God
> Who is our salvation! Selah [pause, and
> calmly think of that]!
>
> Psalm 68:19 (AMPC)

Remember, realize, rejoice—it's not that hard if you think about it. In fact, if you tend to focus on the negative things in life, you could make a sign that says, "Remember—Realize—Rejoice!" Put it somewhere that you will see it often.

Do whatever it takes to help you count your blessings!

Little Things Count

When it comes to loving life, we very often focus on the big things. We think, *I would be so much happier in a different career*, or *If only I could find a spouse, then my life would be so great*, or *When I have more money, or more profitable investments, that's when I can start to relax and enjoy life*. But it's not the big things that often steal our joy—it's the little things.

Think about it: It's the more minor, unexpected things in the course of a day that can cause us to want to pull our hair out. A coffee spill in the car, a slow line at the checkout, a minor disagreement with a coworker, an e-mail that failed to be delivered, a traffic jam on the way to work, a gust of wind that messed up your hair—these are the little things that can put the day on the wrong footing.

But just like a little negativity tries to ruin your day, the little blessings in life can make your day great—it all depends on where your focus is. So when you're counting your blessings, don't just sit passively, waiting for the big blessings to come along…start with the little blessings. A beautiful sunrise, waking up healthy, the joy in a child's giggle, a terrific dinner, a compliment from a friend, a delicious cup of coffee—these blessings add up quickly. It's not just the big things in life that give us joy; the small blessings remind us that we have so much to love about our lives.

> The little blessings in life can make your day great.

Henry David Thoreau said: "An early-morning walk is a blessing for the whole day."[6]

And Mark Twain reminded us: "Humor is mankind's greatest blessing."[7]

These quotes aren't about a booming economy or an elaborate vacation package; they are reminders that peace and joy can be found in the ordinary, inexpensive, overlooked things in life, like a walk or a laugh. It's a wonderful thought: Contentment is often found in the small stuff.

I have found this to be personally true in my life. Over the years, I've learned to slow down and enjoy even the smallest blessings in any given day. A kind word from Dave, a good movie, a compliment from a friend—these "little" things are actually a big deal. These are the things that remind me how blessed I really am.

What about you? What are the everyday blessings you might have overlooked? Do you have friends or family whom you can enjoy a meal with? Is the weather beautiful where you live today? Do you have a bed to sleep in and clean water to drink? (So many in the world don't have either of those things.) Do you have a job that pays the bills? Do you feel good physically today? I ask these questions to remind you that the little things matter! Don't overlook them, and don't take them for granted; these basic blessings are essential to really loving your life.

Blessed to Be a Blessing

Marquis de Lafayette was a politician and French general who was an ally of George Washington in the American Revolution. He was instrumental in helping the colonies win their independence. The story is told that after the war was over, he returned to France and resumed his life as a farmer. He had many estates and there was much work to be done.

In 1783, the harvest in the surrounding region didn't yield many crops. Nearly all of his neighbors suffered as a result of the poor harvest. However, Lafayette's farms were the exception—he did quite well that year. He was able to fill his barns with wheat when the farmers around him could not.

One of his workers thought this was a great time to

take advantage of the opportunity. Seeing how prosperous they had been, he suggested to Lafayette, "This is the time to sell. The bad harvest has raised the price of wheat. We can make a huge profit!" After thinking about the situation and the hungry peasants in the surrounding countryside, the former general disagreed with the profit-making suggestion. Choosing not to maximize his profits at the expense of others, he replied very simply, "No, this is the time to give."[8]

I love this story because it reflects a very biblical attitude: God blesses us in order that we may be a blessing to others. Marquis de Lafayette could have kept all his successful crops to himself, building up his bank account and focusing on his own self-interest. But instead, he chose to help others. We can learn a valuable lesson from his example: The idea of counting our blessings isn't so we can stockpile benefits for ourselves...it's so we can share those blessings with others.

> *The idea of counting our blessings isn't so we can stockpile benefits for ourselves.*

Psalm 21:6 says it this way:

> For You make him most blessed [and a blessing] forever; You make him joyful with the joy of Your presence.

And Philippians 2:4 instructs us:

> Do not merely look out for your own personal interests, but also for the interests of others.

It's a twofold blessing: God blesses you and then He gives you the opportunity to bless others. This is one of the best ways to love your life! Henri Nouwen famously said, "To give someone a blessing is the most significant affirmation we can offer."[9] When you learn to be selfless, sharing your many blessings with those around you, you can't help but have a joyful heart. Generosity is the key to happiness!

As we conclude this chapter, let me encourage you to do two things today:

1. Count the blessings in your life. Remember, it's not just the big things (though they are important). Count the little things, too.
2. Count the ways you can share those blessings with others. Is there a single mom you know who could use a helping hand? Do you know someone who is desperate for some encouragement? Are there needs in your community you could help to meet? Whatever you can do to help, jump in and be a blessing.

God loves you so much that He lavishly pours out His goodness, His peace, His joy, and His blessings on your life. Never forget that. You are loaded down with blessings from Heaven. And with that knowledge look for ways to bless others in return. There is no better time to start than now. Today is a perfect opportunity to help someone else. Think of it this way: *Now is the time to give!*

Don't Forget...

- Here is a great attitude to have: *God has blessed me so much that I can hardly stand it! I'm loaded down with blessings!*
- Many people are living joyless, frustrated lives because they've simply forgotten—or maybe they've never even realized—how blessed they really are.
- When we learn to focus on the good things God has done for us, rather than the trouble or distractions we may be facing, there is absolutely nothing that can steal our joy!
- When you're counting your blessings, don't just sit passively, waiting for the big blessings to come along...start with the little blessings.
- God blesses you and then He gives you the opportunity to bless others. This is one of the best ways to love your life!

No one has ever become poor by giving.

Anne Frank

SECTION II

Love Yourself and You Will Love Your Life

For we are his workmanship, created in Christ Jesus for good works, which God prepared beforehand, that we should walk in them.

Ephesians 2:10 (ESV)

CHAPTER 7

Give Yourself a Break

It is never too late to be what you might have been.

George Eliot

Imagine with me that you are volunteering at a local elementary school. Your schedule opened up and you decided to sign up to lead a reading group and help with crafts for the school's kindergarten class. After about a month, you've learned the names of all the children, you've discovered their cute, individual personalities, and you absolutely love the experience of working with these minds of the future. However, there is one thing that is bothering you...it's little Timmy.

Timmy is an enthusiastic student. He gets along well with his classmates. And he greets you every day with a big hug. Timmy loves school, and you certainly enjoy helping him learn. But Timmy pushes himself so hard to succeed that he becomes easily frustrated with himself.

Some days you find Timmy muttering to himself,

"I wish I was smart like my brother." Other days you see him practicing his letters during recess while the other children are playing games in the schoolyard. And sometimes during class, Timmy will begin to cry if he colors outside the lines or messes up his art project.

You tell him, "It's okay, Timmy. Don't worry; it's not a big deal. We can fix it." But Timmy rarely accepts your encouragement. He wants so badly to do well, to please his parents and impress his teachers, that he internalizes every mistake. Timmy is such a perfectionist that he is unhappy most days. You wonder how a child could put so much pressure on himself. And it breaks your heart when you see him struggling.

I paint that picture for you because I believe it breaks God's heart when He sees you struggling. You're a child of God—He doesn't want you putting so much pressure on yourself. When you make a mistake, lose your temper, forget an appointment—whatever it is—to God, it's the equivalent of coloring outside the lines. You're beating yourself up over it, but God is saying, "It's okay. It's not a big deal. We can fix it." God knows you're not perfect

> God doesn't want you putting so much pressure on yourself.

and He loves and accepts you in your imperfection...
isn't it time you did the same?

I believe one of the best ways to love your life is to
give yourself a break. Do not get angry with yourself
if you occasionally color outside the lines! Of course,
we all want to do our best in our spiritual and personal lives. Yes, we strive to obey the Word of God,
and of course we always want to learn and grow in
Christ every day. But we'll never do any of these things
perfectly. We're all going to make mistakes and occasionally trip in this journey of life. Instead of heaping
pressure on ourselves to live perfectly—then feeling
ashamed and condemned when we don't—we would
be wise to trust God to help us become the best people
He wants us to be.

Philippians 1:6 says this:

> I am convinced and confident of this very
> thing, that He who has begun a good work
> in you will [continue to] perfect and com-
> plete it until the day of Christ Jesus [the
> time of His return].

I love this promise in the Word of God, because
it takes the pressure off. Even though we should try
our best in all areas of our lives, God is the one "who

has begun a good work" in us, and He is the one Who "will [continue to] perfect and complete it until the day of Christ Jesus." So let me encourage you to relax. All that pressure, all that striving to be perfect, all of those self-imposed expectations—take a break and let God help.

Here are four practical ways you can start doing that today:

1. Forgive Yourself When You Mess Up

When I teach the Word of God, one of the things I often do is share illustrations from my own life. I talk about all the times I've messed up and what God has taught me as a result of those mistakes. Sometimes Dave and my children can't believe the things I actually tell in public. I talk about the time I raced a man for the last table at a restaurant (realizing later he was disabled) or the time, early in my life, when I actually stole from my place of employment (years later the Lord instructed me to make restitution). These are just a few of the embarrassing, but true, stories I share.

I do that because I think it's important to realize that *all* of us are going to occasionally miss the mark of perfection. Jesus was the only one Who ever lived a perfect life. You will make mistakes, and I certainly have made my share of mistakes, but when we do,

God has made a way for us to move past our mistakes. We can ask God to forgive us, and we can also forgive ourselves. We can drop it, leave it, and let it go! Say goodbye to it and quickly move on to all the success we will have in the future.

The devil wants to bring condemnation into our lives because condemnation steals our joy. God brings conviction when we sin, but conviction is much different than condemnation. Conviction shows us our faults so we can repent and learn from our mistakes. Condemnation, however, is just meant to bring guilt and shame. It's like a dark cloud hanging over your head, making you feel gloomy and terrible about yourself.

Romans 8:1 tells us:

> Therefore there is now no condemnation
> [no guilty verdict, no punishment] for those
> who are in Christ Jesus.

Isn't that wonderful to know? When you fall short in any area of your life, God never brings condemnation. You are in Christ Jesus, and you have right standing before God because Jesus has already paid for your sins. God has forgiven you, and if you want to love your life, it is important that you receive His forgiveness and, by doing so, forgive yourself.

Take a moment now and think about any event or action that you are still beating yourself up over. It may be something old, it may be something new, it may be something big, it may be something small, and there's a good possibility there are both big and small things that are weighing your heart down. Now I want to encourage you to let those things go. Ask God to forgive you (if you haven't already) and then ask Him to help you forgive yourself. Life becomes so much better when you do.

> You have right standing before God because Jesus has already paid for your sins.

2. Look in the Mirror and Say Something Incredibly Nice About Yourself

I know that may sound silly, but it is important if you are going to live a life that you love. Here is why: We *are* who God says we are, but we *live* according to who *we* say we are. If you think and say you're a failure, a disappointment, or a victim, you are going to start to demonstrate those very traits.

Jesus asked the disciples two questions in Matthew 16. First, He asked, "Who do men say that I am?" After the disciples told Jesus about all the speculation floating around as to who He might be, Jesus asked them, "Who do *you* say that I am?" You may remember this is when Peter proclaimed, "You are the Christ...the Son of the living God" (Matthew 16:16).

Well, I think there is a third question that Jesus is asking us today: *Now that you know Who I am, who do you say that you are?*

That's an important question, because the Bible teaches us that our identity is wrapped up in Christ Jesus. Romans 8:17 says that we are joint heirs with Christ and Philippians 3:9 says that we are found and known in Him. What you say about yourself

> *You are complete, beautiful, whole, and accepted in Christ.*

matters! You are complete, beautiful, whole, and accepted in Christ. I like to say that we are daily becoming what we already are in Christ!

Robert Frost said, "In three words I can sum up everything I've learned about life: It goes on."[10] And as a helpful exercise, I want to ask you: In three words sum up everything you've learned about *yourself* since you've accepted Jesus as your Savior. If you're stuck, let me give you a few suggestions:

- I am loved
- Sin is broken
- God created me

- Forgiven and redeemed
- Life has purpose
- I am valuable
- Unique and treasured

These are just a few examples of things you can say about yourself every day. But don't stop with only three words—that's just meant to get you started. Wake up each day, and say something incredibly nice about yourself...no matter how many words it takes. This isn't some inspirational exercise or self-help technique. This is about speaking the things God has already spoken about you in His Word. When you begin to agree with God about who you are and the future God has for you, there is no way you can't love your life. It's all about perspective, so embrace a godly perspective for your life and never let it go.

I can almost guarantee that you will feel foolish when you first begin to say nice things about yourself. You may even have the mistaken idea that it is wrong or prideful to do so, but it isn't. You are not bragging, you are simply reminding yourself of who you are in Christ, acknowledging the fact that you are His creation and that He has a purpose for you.

3. Walk Away from Negative People and Negative Things

If you sit in the sun all day, you are going to get burned. If you hang out all afternoon in a smoking lounge, you're going to smell like smoke. If you stand in front of a subwoofer at a rock concert, you're likely to damage your hearing. There is just no getting around it. The things you subject yourself to will radically affect you.

In order to really give yourself a break, step away from people or things that bring you discouragement and sour your outlook on life…because they *will* affect you. There are just some people whom we need to love from a distance. If you have family members, friends, or coworkers whose constant negativity drains your joy and saps your peace, you probably need to create some distance. It doesn't mean you don't love them—it just means you need to give yourself a break.

I remember a job Dave had early in his life where his coworkers seemed to have a lot of negativity. At lunch, he didn't want to hear the gossip and complaining about their jobs, so he would spend his lunch listening to Bible teaching and worship music, or just taking a walk and praying. He was kind to his fellow employees during the day and looked for ways to share his faith with them, but when it was break time...he needed a break!

Don't be afraid to give yourself a break, too. Step away from harmful influences or negative talk every chance you get. It's not rude, and it's certainly not pious—it's just smart. If you'll distance yourself from negative, bitter talk and surround yourself with Bible-based, faith-filled influences, your life will become so much more positive.

You may be thinking, *Well Joyce, what if I am married to someone who is extremely negative?* To be clear, I am not suggesting that you get a divorce or leave the marriage because of it, but you still need to give yourself breaks from it as often as possible.

4. Actually Take a Break!

This chapter is titled "Give Yourself a Break," and an important way to do that is to give yourself permission to actually *take a break*.

Everyone deserves a break from time to time. Not only do we deserve it...we need it. *When children are in school, they take breaks from learning so they can play. When musicians are performing, they take breaks to rest. Workers get a lunch break, and*

> Everyone needs a break from time to time.

they often take smaller breaks to get refreshed. When writers are writing, they take breaks to get new ideas. Breaks are crucial. They are healthy times of rest for every level and aspect of life.

If this is true, then why do we run from commitment to commitment, from task to task, without ever stopping to enjoy a break? The reason why so many people are exasperated with their lives is simply because they are exhausted—they haven't recharged their batteries in days, weeks, months, or even years. I must admit that I don't like downtime between appointments and commitments, so I tend to schedule things too close together, and it often causes pressure in my life. I am attempting to learn to love short breaks in-between events. (Pray for me!)

If you started up your car on a hot summer's day and left it running continuously, what would happen? Well, first of all you'd probably run out of gas, but another thing would occur: Your car would overheat. The engine isn't made to run constantly. You'd blow a gasket and might destroy your car in the process.

It's the same way in your own life. If you never stop to rest, you'll run out of gas, overheat, and blow a gasket! This is not the life Jesus came to give you. He wants you to live a life full of

You're not getting any spiritual extra credit with God by running yourself ragged.

peace, joy, contentment, and rest. Remember, in John 10:10, Jesus says: "I came that they may have and enjoy life, and have it in abundance [to the full, till it overflows]." Jesus wants you to love your life!

You're not getting any spiritual extra credit with God by running yourself ragged. Whether you're raising kids, working on a career, going to school, or building a ministry—if you are burning yourself out in the process, your life is going to be far less than what God intended.

Think about this: God rested. Genesis 2:2 says: "And by the seventh day God completed His work which He had done, and He rested (ceased) on the seventh day from all His work which He had done." What an amazing example! God doesn't need to rest, but He did it to give us an example of how we should live. If God rested . . . we should, too.

So look for ways during your day to give yourself a break. Maybe you can unplug your devices and enjoy a cup of coffee. Perhaps you can enjoy a nice dinner with friends. Maybe you simply need to adjust your work schedule so there is room for margin. Maybe you need to take an entire day off! Whatever it is, ask God to help you find ways to relax, refresh, and find joyful rest.

We began this chapter talking about little Timmy, and I want to ask you to consider him once again.

Remember, he was a perfectionist, down on himself when he messed up and generally unhappy from all the internal pressure he was putting on himself. I'm sure if you met little Timmy in real life, you'd want the best for him. You'd remind him that no one is perfect, and you'd encourage him to relax and enjoy all the great things his school day had for him.

Will you give yourself the same advice you'd give Timmy?

Today, when you make a mistake or feel the pressure of expectations, I hope you'll remember that an important part of loving life is learning to give yourself a break. You won't always color perfectly inside the lines, and you may put too much glue on the occasional craft, but it's okay. God is with you, and He helps you correct your mistakes and enjoy every part of your day with Him. This is why life is so great when God is on your side—He began a good work in you and He promises to carry it through to completion.

Don't Forget…

- Instead of heaping pressure on ourselves to live perfectly—then feeling ashamed and condemned when we don't—we would be wise to submit our efforts to God and let Him do the work we've been trying to do the entire time.

- When we sin, God has made a way for us to move past that sin: We can ask God to forgive us, and we can also forgive ourselves.
- God has forgiven you, and if you want to love your life, it is important that you forgive yourself.
- The Word of God teaches us that our identity should be rooted in Christ Jesus. We are new creatures in Him!
- Step away from harmful influences or negative talk every chance you get.
- Look for ways during your day to give yourself a break from the hectic pace of life.

Nothing can stop the man with the right mental attitude from achieving his goal; nothing on Earth can help the man with the wrong mental attitude.

attributed to Thomas Jefferson

CHAPTER 8

"A Little Thing That Makes a Big Difference"

If you don't like something, change it. If you can't change it, change your attitude.

Maya Angelou

One of the most important, life-changing things I have learned over the years as I've studied the Word of God is the importance of attitude. It may be a little thing, but it makes a huge difference in almost every area of our lives. Sometimes the tiniest attitude adjustment can change an entire day. No one can make us have a bad attitude if we don't want to, and no circumstance can make us have a bad attitude if we don't want to. Your attitude belongs to you, and it is a determining factor in how much you will be able to love your life. A negative, doubtful, complaining attitude is a quick way to lose your love for life. However, a positive, hope-filled, optimistic attitude can turn around any bad day!

I read about a widow who had two sons. She

depended on her sons for financial support. One of her sons was in the umbrella business. So the first thing the mother did each morning was look outside to see if it was going to rain. On days when it was cloudy and overcast, she was in high spirits. *It might rain and my son will be able to sell a lot of umbrellas!* But if the sun was shining when she looked out of her window, she would be instantly depressed because no umbrellas would be sold that day.

The widow's other son had a very different profession—he sold fans. So every day that it looked like it might rain, she would be so upset. *It's too cloudy; no fans will be sold today!* However, if it was bright and sunny, she would be in a much better mood because there was a chance the heat of the sun would convince customers to buy a fan.

As you can see, regardless of the weather, this woman always had something to worry and be upset about.

One day, while complaining to a friend about the weather, her friend made the unmistakable observation, "Cheer up! You've got nothing to be upset about. If the sun is shining, people will buy fans, and if it rains, they'll buy umbrellas instead. Just change your attitude. You can't lose."[11]

This simple anecdote reminds me of the way so many people live (and the way I lived for a lot of years).

It's very easy to go through life seeing the negative in every situation. But when we live with this negativity, it's impossible to love and enjoy our lives. If all we see are the problems, the hassles and the cloudy skies in the world around us, we won't love our lives, because we will be focused on all that we think is wrong, and the negativity will act like a huge sponge, soaking up any joy and enjoyment we might have had.

I've discovered that the right attitude can make any situation better. It doesn't really matter what is happening on the outside…what matters is what is happening on the inside. Joy and peace are the result of a godly, faith-filled attitude. A good attitude is not automatic in our lives; it must be chosen daily!

> A good attitude is not automatic in our lives; it must be chosen daily!

I love to be around people who have positive and hopeful attitudes. Their optimism can be contagious. They remind me that happiness is not dictated by our circumstances—it is fostered by the attitudes of our hearts. This is one of the main reasons I decided years ago to work with God to change my negative attitude and outlook. It wasn't always easy—I definitely needed God's help—but the more I studied the Word of God, the more I saw that a positive attitude is God's will for our lives.

Philippians 2:14 (AMPC) says:

> Do all things without grumbling and fault-finding and complaining [against God] and questioning and doubting [among yourselves].

Philippians 4:8 says:

> Whatever is true, whatever is honorable and worthy of respect, whatever is right and confirmed by God's word, whatever is pure and wholesome, whatever is lovely and brings peace, whatever is admirable and of good repute; if there is any excellence, if there is anything worthy of praise, think continually on these things [center your mind on them, and implant them in your heart].

These are just two of the countless "attitude" Scriptures in the Bible. If we will study and obey them, we'll finally be able to defeat that negativity and discouragement that swirls around us. We'll be able to live a life in Christ that we really love!

Attitude of Obedience

When we talk about attitude, most people immediately think of disposition—a smiling face, a cheerful persona, or a positive outlook on life. These things are symptoms of a good attitude, but attitude goes even deeper than that. Our attitude is very often our decision on how we are going to live. That's why I think an attitude of obedience to God is so very important if you are going to really follow and enjoy the path God has laid out for you.

As Christians, every single one of us has been called to be obedient to God in big things and little things, day in and day out. Living in godly obedience is sometimes challenging, but God has empowered and equipped us for the job. We can do whatever we need to do with His help—and not only that, we can learn to do it with smiles on our faces!

The thing so very few people realize is that when you develop an attitude of total obedience to God, you find His good and perfect will. He gives us instructions, not to harm us or keep us from happiness— the exact opposite is true. His guidance in our lives is for our benefit. He knows what is best for each one of

> *When you develop an attitude of total obedience to God, you find His good and perfect will.*

us, and He directs us in those paths. God is never trying to take anything away from us, but He does often guide us to change things in our lives that are blocking His blessings. When we are prompted to obey, our lives just get better and better.

God wants to give you instructions about the biggest decisions in life or in the minor day-to-day details. For example, maybe you're shopping and the Holy Spirit nudges you to pick up the trash that is on the floor. You aren't the one who dropped it, but you feel the urging of the Lord to pick it up. Or maybe God puts a desire in your heart to give a gift to someone...and it's a person you don't even like! At other times, God may ask you to stick with a job or a situation that you'd rather run away from while He finishes His work in you. All of these examples are perfect times to demonstrate an attitude of obedience.

It takes a decision on your part to be obedient to God. When God doesn't give you what you want, it's easy to pout, feel sorry for yourself, or act angry and upset. This is when you must decide to discipline yourself to keep doing what God has commanded, even though your flesh wants to do the exact opposite. There may be times you want to ignore God and just do your own thing, but if you really understand that God has your best interest at heart and say, "Lord, I know You are guiding me into what is best for my life, and I'm going to be obedient today," He will give you the supernatural strength and joy to follow through and do what He is guiding you to do.

Are you aware of any area of disobedience to God in your life? If so, then repent and make decisions in line with God's will. Even if the area God has dealt with you about is a little thing, do what He tells you to do. Remember, little things can make a big difference in your life.

Maybe you feel stuck right now, as if things just aren't moving along in your life. Perhaps you said no to God at some point on your journey, and you need to go back to that place and be obedient. For example, if you need to forgive someone who has hurt or offended you, but you haven't done it because you thought you could just move on with God's plan, I can tell you from personal experience that it won't work.

When we do the right things and are quick to obey God to the best of our ability, we may not see the benefits right away, but we will in due time. If we do the part that God asks us to do, He will never fail to do His part! Develop an attitude of obedience, and He will bless you in ways you can't even begin to imagine. And while you are waiting, you will sleep better at night because your conscience will be clear.

Attitude of Hope

It is so important to have hope for your future. Rather than expecting disappointing or negative things to happen, ask God to help you develop an attitude of hope!

I grew up in a very negative, hopeless environment. I lived in an abusive atmosphere with negative people, alcoholism, fear, violence, and anger. The result was that I developed an attitude that said, *It is better to expect nothing good than to expect good things and be disappointed when they don't happen.* Have you ever found yourself wondering, *What else can go wrong?* Well, this was my mind-set. I was programmed to think, *What bad thing is going to happen next?* This attitude of hopelessness followed me into my adult life.

But through the years, God began to speak to my heart about this. He showed me that He wanted me to have hope that good things were going to happen, instead of always assuming the worst. Jeremiah 29:11 tells us that God's thoughts and plans for us are "for peace and well-being and not for disaster, to give you a future and a hope."

God wanted me to say, "Something good is going to happen!" And He wants you to develop the exact same attitude. God wants you to live a life of hope, because this is a life you will love.

The truth is, God doesn't work in us through negative attitudes full of self-pity, laziness, passivity, or an everybody-owes-me perspective. Those are destructive mind-sets from the enemy. No good thing will ever come from those attitudes. God works through faith! He wants us to have faith that His promises are going to be fulfilled in our lives. But before we can have faith, we have to have hope. This is why an attitude of hope is so very important.

> God wants you to live a life of hope, because this is a life you will love.

I love to teach about hope, live with hope, and share hope with those around me. The reason is simple: Hope is a powerful and life-enriching gift from God. If you're wondering what exactly hope is, the answer is simple: Hope is a favorable and confident expectation; it's an expectant attitude that something good is going to happen and things will work out, no matter what situation we're facing.

One of my favorite verses in the Bible is Zechariah 9:12 (AMPC). Here is what it says:

> Return to the stronghold [of security and prosperity], you prisoners of hope; even today do I declare that I will restore double your former prosperity to you.

I like that phrase "prisoners of hope." When you're a prisoner of hope, you are so convinced about the power of hope that you just cannot do anything but hope for things to improve. And when times are frustrating or you're dealing with disappointment, an attitude of hope will prevent you from thinking and saying negative things.

Hope is an attitude that will inspire and empower you to love your life. And this is why God wants us to be locked up in hope. He wants us to have an attitude that trusts Him no matter what—an attitude that believes He can change what needs to be changed and that all things are possible with Him. If we will dedicate ourselves to having an attitude of hope, there is no way we can lose.

Embrace a New Attitude Today

I want to encourage you not to waste another day with a defeated, discouraged, woe-is-me attitude. Ask God to help you see what attitude changes you need to make, and then go about the process of developing a godly attitude and outlook for your life. I'm passionate about this, because as I learned to change my attitude in obedience to God's Word, my life became so much better. And I know yours will, too. So what are you waiting for? Embrace a new attitude today!

Don't Forget...

- A positive, hope-filled, optimistic attitude can turn around any bad day.
- Every one of us has been called to be obedient to God in big things and little things, day in and day out.
- God's guidance in our lives is for our benefit. He knows what is best for each one of us, and He directs us in that path.
- Instead of expecting disappointing or negative things to happen, ask God to help you develop an attitude of hope.
- When you're a prisoner of hope, you are surrounded by a confident expectation of good.

The hardest challenge is to be yourself in a world where everyone else is trying to make you be somebody else.

E. E. Cummings

CHAPTER 9

Let's Get Spontaneous

I'd rather die on an adventure than live standing still.

V. E. Schwab

The crowds were especially large that day. The exact count wasn't reported—just "a very large crowd." Picture the enormous hoard of people at a state fair or a massive rally with inestimable numbers. It must have been something like this, because the size of the pressing throng caused Jesus to do something differently that day—it was a move no one saw coming.

As the growing mass of people, desperate to hear His teaching, pressed Jesus closer and closer to the water's edge, the disciples must have wondered, *What are we going to do? There's no more room!* Peter may have said to Andrew, or James might have whispered to John, "He's going to have to send them all home. This crowd is pushing Him right into the sea."

The problem was evident to all. The swelling mass of people gathered near the Sea of Galilee to hear from this new rabbi was running of out room. Jesus was a huge draw, and the crowd was just too big that day. Jesus had run out of real estate. He was being pushed up against the sea. This was a problem no one anticipated (except Jesus) and one that was quickly becoming a cause of concern. That's when Jesus did something...unusual. Luke 5:1–3 paints the picture:

> Now it happened that while Jesus was standing by the Lake of Gennesaret (Sea of Galilee), with people crowding all around Him and listening to the word of God; that He saw two boats lying at the edge of the lake, but the fishermen had gotten out of them and were washing their nets.
>
> He got into one of the boats, which was Simon's, and asked him to put a little distance from the shore. And He sat down and began teaching the crowds from the boat.

Instead of going the obvious route and settling on a solution everyone saw coming, like building a stage, setting up a security perimeter, or sending the crowd away, Jesus did something different—He preached from a boat.

The people needed to hear the Word and His usual method of preaching simply wasn't going to work that day, so instead of giving up, Jesus did something that He did not usually do. I recall doing something unusual also in order to get the Word to the people waiting to hear it.

I was in Cambodia and the crowd had gathered inside the arena. Just as I was ready to go across the street from my hotel to the meeting, I received a phone call saying that a government official who was against Christianity had managed to pull some strings with the staff at the arena and he had the power shut off. We would have no sound, but even worse, an electric gate had been closed, keeping the people inside and keeping me out!

Some time went by and it became obvious that I was not going to get into the arena in the usual way. Should I give up or do something spontaneous that I had never done before? I asked if there was any way at all that I could get in, and my son said that there was a high fence in the back, and if I was bold enough to climb on top of the trash containers, I could be lifted over the fence. I didn't even hesitate; I went for it, and although I had to preach that night through a handheld megaphone instead of a microphone, I did it. The worship team sang, and I brought a message about determination and never giving up. The crowd was very stirred by the example I had set. Actually, the entire city ended up talking about it, and I think it ended up better than if we had done things the usual way. By the way, I was at least sixty-five years old when I did it!

Recently a woman named Louise, who was 102 years old, attended one of my conferences. She had attended her first one when she was 100, and she liked it so much that she wanted to come back. She sat in every session and took notes. She told our team that she watched my television program each day. They interviewed her and asked why she liked the ministry so much, and she replied, "Well, Joyce just has such a sense of adventure!" I think what she was really saying was that watching the program was helping to keep her young, alert, and active. She wanted to keep her sense of adventure and obviously did not have an attitude that she was too old to do anything anymore. She seemed to me to be more enthusiastic about life than many thirty-year-olds I encounter, and I firmly believe it was the result of her attitude. I was personally very blessed and encouraged by her. I hope we all keep the same kind of attitude however long we live.

This brief story about Jesus preaching from a boat is made up of three verses in the Gospel of Luke and just one verse in Mark's account (Mark 4:1), but I love this decision by Jesus because I believe it shows us so much. It gives us three important things about His nature to consider:

- Jesus refused to give up!
- Jesus used what He had (a boat) instead of being defeated by what He didn't have.
- Every day with Jesus was an adventure.

Following the example of Jesus is about following the pattern and actions of His life. We should follow His model of prayer, we should heed His example of service, we should learn from His demonstration of kindness...but that's not all. We can also follow other behaviors He demonstrated: laughter, unpredictability, an enjoyment of life...and spontaneity. Don't be so busy making a living that you forget to make a life that is filled with memories.

> Don't be so busy making a living that you forget to make a life that is filled with memories.

Surprise Some People...Including Yourself

One of the biggest reasons people stop loving their lives is because life becomes stale, predictable, and boring. Every day is the same: Get up, take the kids to school, run the same errands as last week, go to the exact same grocery store and buy food for the exact same meals, watch the same TV shows...I'm getting bored just thinking about it. It's like the old cartoon series *Pinky and the Brain*, where Pinky would ask Brain, "What are we going to do tonight, Brain?" Then Brain would predictably reply, "The same thing we do every night, Pinky...try to take over the world." Even something as ambitious as world domination can become routine if it's the same thing you do *every* night.

Jesus was anything but predictable—He stopped funeral processions, He showed up at a wedding and turned water into wine, He talked to the outcast, He dined with sinners...and He preached from a boat. Plain and simple: Jesus was spontaneous.

If you want to find a fun way to love your life, this is a wonderful example to follow. God didn't create you to live a dull, boring, routine, predictable life. He created you to live life to the fullest. He wants you to get the most out of every day.

What are some things you could do today to break up the monotony of routine? What are some actions that could shake you out of the boredom trap? It doesn't have to be a huge, grand event...joy can be found in the small things, too. What if you decided to:

- Take a different way to work
- Eat something you have never eaten before
- Enjoy lunch at work with someone you have never spent time with

- Try a different hairstyle (even if just for a day or two)
- Wear a color that is not conservative (if you normally play it safe)
- Stop being afraid of what people will think and follow your heart

If you do any of these things (or others that you come up with on your own) I'll bet the people in your life will be surprised—and so will you! Spontaneity is a fun way to make the most of the life God has given you!

> *Spontaneity is a fun way to make the most of the life God has given you!*

Let me be clear: Being spontaneous doesn't mean being irresponsible. We all have daily obligations and responsibilities that aren't always the most exciting. However, just because we have to meet expectations at work or home that aren't always thrilling, that doesn't mean we have to lead boring lives. There is still plenty of margin in our days to do something fun and surprising. Set a goal to do something out of the ordinary at least once a month, and I think you will have fun planning it.

Don't settle for safe, routine, and boring. Look for ways to surprise yourself and others today.

Use What You Have in New and Unexpected Ways

When I talk about things like "living a life of adventure" or "finding the joy in being spontaneous," people sometimes say, "Well, I can't do that because I don't have enough resources or enough time." But I think it's interesting that Jesus used what He had on hand (a docked boat) to do something different. I used what I had when I couldn't preach in my usual way—a trash container, a few strong men to lift me over a fence, and a megaphone!

Jesus certainly could have walked on water (He demonstrated that supernatural wonder in Matthew 14), but instead, He showed us this principle of using what you have.

This isn't the only time in the Gospels Jesus demonstrates this truth. In Mark 6, a crowd of five thousand men (plus women and children) had gathered to listen to Jesus teach. As the day went on, the crowd grew hungry. Once again, the disciples were faced with a dilemma. *No one wants to have to deal with a hungry crowd!* When the disciples came to Jesus with this problem, they assumed Jesus would send the crowd home, but He had a different idea. He asked,

"What do you have?"

The answer wasn't very impressive at first

glance—all they had was a boy's lunch made up of five loaves of bread and two fish. But that was more than enough in the hands of God! Jesus gave thanks, broke the bread, and the multitude was fed. Jesus took what they had and used it to do something incredible.

Can you imagine the conversation around the campfire that night among the disciples? *I can't believe what God did today. I didn't think what we had was nearly enough. It was amazing to see what Jesus can do with the little we have! What we have will always be enough with God on our side!*

> It's amazing to see what Jesus can do with the little we have!

When God called Moses to lead the Israelites out of Egypt into the Promised Land, Moses went on and on about what he didn't have and couldn't do, but God asked him, "What do you have in your hand?" Moses had a staff, an ordinary shepherd's stick, but God used it to do mighty miracles, like part the Red Sea and bring water out of a rock.

To spontaneously love your life, you don't have to have more—you have to be creative about using what you do have. What you have is more than enough. God has already provided what you need to live a refreshing, routine-shattering life!

- Use your talent in a new way.
- Be creative in your budget so you can have an exciting new adventure (it doesn't have to be expensive).
- Start doing some of the things you see other people do that you have always wanted to do, but have not done because it hasn't been part of your normal routine.

You've been given so much from God already. Simply ask Him today to show you how to maximize what you already have. Your resources, your time schedule, your gifts and talents—God can do something incredible with it all.

Reach for Something New

When was the last time you did something for the first time? In other words, have you been trapped in sameness for so long that life has become dull? You weren't created to live a passive life that never reaches for new challenges, new opportunities, and new adventures with God. It is very easy to keep doing the same old familiar things, but they don't present any challenges and they don't demand that we use our creative skills. Doing something new requires that we stretch our faith and ourselves in areas that may initially be uncomfortable, but that eventually give us a great story to tell. My story about climbing the fence is a great story, but I had to do it before I could tell the story.

Decide to Have Some Fun

As Christians, we spend a lot of time talking about the deep, spiritual issues of life, and that's good because those things are important. But it's not good if that is all we ever talk about. A good friend of mine said that he became so serious about everything in life after becoming a Christian that his wife woke him up one night and said, "Are you ever going to make me laugh again?"

Thankfully, it was a wake-up call for him, and he made a change.

I hope you'll take this away from this chapter: Sometimes the most spiritual thing you can do is look for ways to laugh and do something new. God is not boring and He doesn't want us to be boring, either. Don't get so bogged down with the serious issues of life

> *Sometimes the most spiritual thing you can do is look for ways to laugh and do something new.*

that you forget to stop and actually enjoy your life. Get spontaneous today—trust me, you'll love it!

Don't Forget...

- Jesus demonstrated a life of laughter, unpredictability, joy...and spontaneity.
- Being spontaneous doesn't mean being irresponsible.
- Don't settle for safe, routine, and boring. Look for ways to surprise yourself and others today.
- You don't need something more to start being spontaneous; you just need to start using what you do have.

Thou hast made us for thyself, O Lord, and our heart is restless until it finds its rest in thee.

Augustine of Hippo

CHAPTER 10

Enjoy the Season You're In

I believe that God puts us in this jolly world to be happy.

Robert Baden-Powell

Ask any group of people what their favorite season is and you'll get a variety of different answers with compelling reasons why.

Some people love the heat of summer. They can't wait for the sun to be shining down so they can get outdoors and enjoy the pool or the beach, or just drink a lemonade on a hot summer's day. Others absolutely hate summer. They prefer the cold of winter. To these people, a brisk winter's day is absolute heaven. They can't wait to see snow fall, they listen to Christmas music all year long, and they get absolutely giddy at the thought of a fire in the fireplace on a cold winter's night.

Of course, there are a lot of people who are convinced fall is the greatest of the seasons. The leaves are changing and the temperature is perfect most days. For them, fall means football is back and school is in session—*What could be better than that?* Last, there are those who live for the spring. They love the fact that the flowers are blooming and the harshness of winter is over. Spring means Easter, fresh starts, and pastel colors. For spring lovers, this is as good as it gets, and they won't let you convince them otherwise!

(My favorite season is fall. What's yours?)

Although fall is my favorite, I can be happy and find things to enjoy in each season, and hopefully you can also. It would be a shame to only enjoy a portion of each year and be miserable during the rest of it.

I mention this because just as the calendar is made up of seasons, our lives are made up of seasons, too. I'm talking about the general phases or divisions of our lives. These seasons are different for each of us, but they sometimes look like this:

- A season of study, where academics are the focus.
- A season of raising young children, with diapers, teething, late nights, and lots of crying.
- A season of waiting—a time when you're waiting for God to answer a prayer regarding health, career, relationships, and so on. Or a time when one season has ended and you're waiting for God to bring the next one to you.

- A season of increased work while you start a business or a ministry, or just engage in a new career.
- A season of spiritual learning. A time of intense study of the Word, receiving new instruction or correction from God, going deeper in your faith.
- We have seasons of sowing and seasons of reaping. Sowing usually means we are sacrificing something for the hope of a future reward, and harvest is when the reward finally comes.

These are just a few examples; of course, there are many more. And much like the calendar, we often decide which seasons we love...and which seasons we intensely dislike. I can't tell you how many times someone has told me, "I just can't wait for this season to be over." That statement is a telltale sign that they are *not* enjoying the season they are in. The good news is that even if you don't enjoy the particular season you are in, you can make a decision to still enjoy your life in the midst of it.

I understand that some seasons can be difficult, but if we find joy only in certain seasons, we are missing out on God's best during all the other seasons. God

> God wants you to have joy in every single season of your life.

doesn't want you to just love your life *some* of the time, during *particular* seasons or situations. God wants you to have joy in every single season of your life. No matter how difficult that season may appear at the time, God has something good for you in it, and I encourage you to look for it. One good thing I have learned about every season is that it is used by God to prepare me for the next one.

When my ministry was very small and stayed that way for a number of years, I thought that season would never end. It was a difficult time for me because I had big dreams, not small ones. Eventually the ministry grew and became an international outreach, and I now realize that most of the preparation I needed for where I am now took place in those first years when everything was small. The ministry didn't grow, but I grew spiritually, and God worked many good changes in my character that I needed in order to be where I am now.

The apostle Paul said in Philippians 4:11 (AMPC),

> I have learned how to be content (satisfied to the point where I am not disturbed or disquieted) in whatever state I am.

In this verse of Scripture, Paul is describing an amazing life. He had learned to love his life no matter what the season. Whether he was in a season of learning, a season of trial, a season of plenty or one of lack, a season of travel, a season of waiting, or a season of successful ministry—Paul said, "I am content."

God wants the same thing for you today. In whatever season you are in, God wants you to know that you can find peace and contentment. Don't waste your days thinking, *I'll be happy* when…When *this is over*…When *I get to the next level in my career*…When *the kids grow up*…When *my spouse starts appreciating me*…

Even though it may not always be easy, you can enjoy your life *now*. It is just one decision away! Because most of your ability to enjoy life is found in your attitude toward what is happening, rather than your circumstances. You can learn to rely on God and find peace and contentment today, no matter what season you are in.

How Do You Feel About Your Job?

Let's just start off by getting right to the practical heart of the matter: your job. There is a quote attributed to Confucius that says, "Choose a job you love, and you will never have to work a day in your life."[12] While that sounds good, there is a problem with that quote: Most people don't have a job they love. In fact, in a Gallup poll done several years ago, 70 percent of respondents said they hate their jobs.[13] It's hard to live a life you love if you're going to a job you hate every day. So, if you're in a difficult job situation during this season of your life, let me make a suggestion...

Work for the Lord...not just for your employer.

If you don't like your employer or your current job, it can be very difficult to have the right attitude. I know this firsthand. I've had plenty of jobs where I wanted to pull my hair out. I would go home many days and pray, "God, I can't take this anymore. These people don't appreciate the work I'm doing. Surely this job is not the right one for me!" If you've felt the same way, let me remind you what the Word of God says. Colossians 3:23 give us a powerful instruction:

> Whatever you do [whatever your task may be], work from the soul [that is, put in your very best effort], as [something done] for the Lord and not for men.

Notice that Paul didn't say, *If you like your job, put in your very best effort for the Lord*, or *When it's a good day in the office...*, or even, *If your boss is a good person...* No, the Word of God says very clearly, "**Whatever** you do... [put in your very best effort], as [something done] for the Lord."

If we will live in obedience to this verse of Scripture, it can be very freeing. When you go to work each day, planning to have the best attitude and work ethic you can because you are working for the Lord, it changes your entire perspective. Now it doesn't matter what your coworkers do or how rude the boss may be...because you aren't working for them. You are doing your work in a way that pleases God.

If you'll determine to have that mind-set, something truly incredible happens. The very next verse (Colossians 3:24) goes on to say:

> Knowing [with all certainty] that it is from the Lord [not from men] that you will receive the inheritance which is your [greatest] reward. It is the Lord Christ whom you [actually] serve.

Wow! Your reward, your inheritance, your joy from a job well done—it all comes from God. He sees your hard work, and He knows the frustrations you feel on the job. But if you'll decide to do your best with a godly attitude, He is going to bless you, and He may just bless you with a better job than you could have ever imagined. I don't think God is inclined to give us more if we are already complaining about what we have. Be thankful and happy where you are and ask God for what you want. He hears your prayers and will give you your heart's desire if you continue delighting yourself in Him in your present circumstance.

True promotion comes from God (see Psalm 75:-6–7). Your times are in His hands, and you can be content while you wait for change.

Stepping Out into the Unknown

Although I don't recommend doing foolish things or getting ahead of God's timing in your life, it is possible that at some point you may need to take a leap of faith if you are ever going to get where you want to be.

One of the reasons people hate their jobs is because they have to keep doing them to earn money, rather than because they truly believe they are fulfilling their destiny. I would rather have less money and more joy than lots of money with misery. Wouldn't you?

I am not suggesting that you be irresponsible, but walking by faith always means there will come a time when you need to step into the unknown. You may wonder what will happen if you are wrong, as we all do. But we must not be so afraid of

> *We must not be so afraid of doing the wrong thing that we never do anything.*

doing the wrong thing that we never do anything. A little adventure never hurt anybody, and if you take a step and find out you did the wrong thing, you can always backtrack and start again. I tried to go on television several years before it was the right time, and it was a total failure. I went back to doing what I was doing, and at the perfect time God opened the right door for me to be on television again, and it worked!

There are very few mistakes that cannot be corrected, except never being willing to make one. That is the biggest mistake we can make and one that may cost us the best future we could have had. When God called Joshua to lead the Israelites across the Jordan and into the Promised Land, He told him they should follow the Ark that represented God's presence to them, because they had not passed that way before (see Joshua 3:3–4). Just as they did, when we step out into the unknown, we need to follow God to the best of our ability and trust that He will lead us. I believe that even if we get on a wrong path, God will guide us back onto the right one if our trust is in Him.

To sum it up let me say this: If you hate your job, you can do one of two things. You can get a new attitude and stay where you are, or you can make a change if you sense God leading you to do that. But merely keeping a job and hating it is not a viable option!

Learning to Be Content

Learning to be content is really an essential key to learning to love your life. This is true in your job... but it's also true in *everything* else. Olympic gold medalist Kristin Armstrong said, "No one can steal contentment, joy, gratitude or peace—we have to give it away."[14] She's right about that, but the sad thing is we give those things away all the time. The moment something goes wrong or a challenge presents itself, we may become discouraged and disheartened, giving our peace and contentment away. To be content does not mean that we don't desire change, but it does mean that we can enjoy where we are on the way to where we are going. Having faith and hope in Jesus helps us believe that even if today is difficult, tomorrow will be better.

Choosing to be content is something we learn. I wasted many years being discontent and upset. Thankfully I finally realized that I wasn't making anything better but I was making myself miserable. Even Paul said in Philippians 4:11, that he had "learned" how to be content.

I wanted to learn to love and enjoy the life Jesus came to give me, and I got to the point I wanted it so badly that I was willing to do whatever it took. I wanted to be at peace no matter what was going on

around me. Do you want the same thing? If so, begin
by saying:

> God, I desire Your contentment and Your
> joy so much that I am willing to let go of my
> old attitudes and mind-sets. I want to love
> my life with You no matter what season I
> am in. I trust that You are teaching me and
> developing my character in this season.

The Amplified Bible (Classic Edition) defines the
word "content" as "satisfied to the point where I am
not disturbed or disquieted in whatever state I am."
This is a great definition, because it does not say that
I must be satisfied to the point where I don't ever
want change, but I can be satisfied to the point that I
am not anxious or disturbed.

One of the main ways to find contentment in the
midst of something that we don't particularly enjoy is
to stop focusing continually on what we do not like.
The more we think about how much we dislike our
job, or the people we work with, or anything else for
that matter, the more discontented we become. If I
have a pain anywhere in my body, all of my attention
tends to go toward it, but if I get it off of my mind,
it seems less intense. Yesterday my back was hurting,
but I went shopping with my daughter and I found

two blouses that I *really* liked, and I realized later that while I was excited about the blouses, I didn't seem to notice the pain. Although I cannot spend all my time shopping to divert my attention from pain, I can go ahead and live my life and enjoy it while God is taking care of my problem.

We can choose what we want to think about, and the thoughts we choose affect every area of our lives, especially our emotions. A happy life requires happy and hope-filled thoughts. God's Word teaches us that a happy heart does us good like a medicine (see Proverbs 17:22).

> A happy life requires happy and hope-filled thoughts.

I have come to believe that being content is one of the greatest ways we can glorify God. So make the decision today to be content in the season you are in while you are waiting for the next season God has for you. Trust God: Don't wait until everything is perfect before you decide to enjoy your life.

Don't Forget...

- Just as the calendar is made up of seasons, our lives are made up of seasons, too.
- God doesn't want you to just love your life *some* of the time—during *particular* seasons or

situations. He wants you to be content in every season of life.

- It doesn't matter what your coworkers do or how rude the boss may be…because you aren't working for them. You are doing your work for God, in a way that pleases Him.
- Don't wait until everything is perfect before you decide to enjoy your life. Remember that God has your very best interest at heart, and be content regardless of your circumstances.

People become attached
to their burdens
sometimes more than
the burdens are attached
to them.

George Bernard Shaw

CHAPTER 11

Rediscover Your Life

Life is 10 percent what happens to you and 90 percent how you react to it.

Charles R. Swindoll

I once read that the great American actor Marlon Brando had a very bad sense of direction. This dated back to his childhood. The story is told that he wandered aimlessly so much on his way to kindergarten class, his sister eventually had to take him to class on a leash.

It's a pretty funny picture when it comes to kindergarten, but it's not so funny when it comes to life. Unfortunately, many of us, like Marlon Brando, are wandering aimlessly. We feel lost—lost in our relationships, lost in our faith, and generally lost in life. We can let our circumstances become a leash that determines and controls the direction we take. At one time, we had a plan and we knew where we were going, but it seems like at some point in time, we lost our way.

The good news is that if you are a Christian, you

have been given the Holy Spirit. The Holy Spirit is many things for us—He is a Comforter, a Counselor, and a Friend—but one of the most important things He is for us is a Guide.

John 16:13 tells us: "But when He, the Spirit of Truth, comes, He will guide you into all the truth [full and complete truth]." And Romans 8:14 says: "For all who are allowing themselves to be led by the Spirit of God are sons of God."

These verses remind us that the Holy Spirit is always available to steer us through life. We never have to feel lost again. The Holy Spirit guides us so we can discover—and, if need be, rediscover—God's plan and purpose for our lives. I think the very best way to love your life is to let the Holy Spirit be your guide each day. You can embrace the adventure of a life lived with and for God!

> The Holy Spirit is always available to steer us through life.

If you feel lost or confused, if it seems like life has gotten away from you a little bit, if you don't have nearly the amount of joy you used to have, I want to encourage you today: You can rediscover your life! You can go back to the place where you got lost and move forward from there. Don't settle for merely existing. Press toward the goal of experiencing the life that Jesus truly wants you to have.

Reject Stress and Rediscover
the Joy of Peace

Stress is one of the main culprits that steals our joy and derails our lives from the path God has for us. I know firsthand what it's like to live under the pressure of stress, and I know what it's like to have God's peace. I have come to a point in my life where I can honestly say that I will do whatever I have to do to have God's peace in my life. And the reason is simple: It is not God's will for us to live with stress all the time. Perhaps somewhere along the way you lost your peace due to a tragedy or trial in your life and you need to rediscover what it is like to be peaceful.

It's easy for us to feel like we can't avoid being stressed-out because it's just the way the world is today. There is an epidemic of stress in our culture—everywhere we turn there seems to be something else to worry or be anxious about. Hectic schedules, catastrophe in the news, economic downturns—it's all very stressful. But just because stress is the new normal in our world, that doesn't mean we have to adopt the ways of our culture and live the same way.

We have two options: We can continue to be stressed, anxious, worried, and miserable, or we can learn to rediscover and recapture our peace.

Jesus said in John 14:27,

Peace I leave with you; My [perfect] peace I give to you; not as the world gives do I give to you. Do not let your heart be troubled, nor let it be afraid. [Let My perfect peace calm you in every circumstance and give you courage and strength for every challenge.]

Recently I went through several weeks of turmoil involving lots of different things. Surgery, pressure regarding an important decision that needed to be made, a heavy work schedule, a flood in our area, and roof damage from storms, and the list could go on and on. I recall saying to God, "I feel like I have gotten off track and lost sight of the most important thing in my life, and that is You!"

It seemed as if I was lost in a maze and was trying to find my way back home. Have you ever felt that way? Do you perhaps feel that way right now? God showed me that I needed to calm my soul and ask Him to guide me back to where I needed to be. My soul was filled with frustration and turmoil, and He guided me back to peace. He wants to do the same thing for you anytime you need it, but it will involve being obedient to make the changes He guides you to make.

Being set free from the pressure of stress begins with understanding John 14:27 and living in obedience to it. It is important we understand that if we are going to discover or rediscover how to love our lives, we will have to *let God* change the things we cannot change and do the things we cannot do. We cannot continue allowing ourselves to be upset and disturbed and have peace at the same time. We can have one or the other, but we cannot simultaneously have both.

The first thing we can do is pray and be willing to hear what God has to say about the real root of our stressful problem. If you're already doing your part—evaluating your schedule, letting go of negativity, and refusing to worry—then simply let go and trust that God will fix things. But if you are convicted of any area in your life that needs to change, ask God to help you make the change and be willing to do whatever you need to do in order to have peace. Remember, Jesus gives us *His* peace—not as the world gives, but His own special peace. His peace functions *in* the storms of life rather than waiting until they are over and life is bright and sunny once again.

Pray and obey! To pray and obey means we make a commitment not to live based on the culture around us but by the leading of the Holy Spirit, who lives in us as born-again believers in Christ. Our mind-set should be: *With God's help, I'm ready to make a change.* Then as we do what God shows us to do (or what He shows us not to do), we'll be able to rediscover the joy of living a life in relationship with God.

Think a New Way in Order to
Live a New Way

When we take time to renew our minds with God's Word, we learn how to think like God thinks, say what God says, and act like He wants us to act. This is the key to learning to love our lives! Although I know and have experienced the benefits of thinking properly, that does not mean that I always do it. At times, I have to rediscover the power of right thinking! I realize I have gotten off the right path, but thankfully, I can always get back on the right one by making a decision to do so.

You may wonder, *How do I discover a new way to think?*

There are literally thousands of thoughts that run through our minds every day, so how do we control all of them? The first thing we need to believe is that it is possible to do so with God's help. I talked with a woman recently who was reading my book *Battlefield of the Mind,* and she said, "It is getting harder and harder for me to keep reading it." I asked if that meant that she wasn't enjoying it, and she said, "Oh no, I am enjoying it, but the more I read, the more

I realize I need to change, and the more difficult it becomes to keep thinking the way I always have in the past." She was learning a new way of thinking and being challenged by the Holy Spirit to be obedient to do it.

For example, many people think it's normal to worry, and this woman had done a lot of worrying in her life, but as a Christian, worrying is not a normal way of thinking. Philippians 4:6 says, "Do not be anxious or worried about anything." Of course, this doesn't mean we won't ever deal with feelings of concern or worry, but when we do, we can pray and give them to God so we can have His peace while we go through a hard time. This is the life God wants you to discover if you have never had it, or to rediscover it if you have lost it!

1 Corinthians 2:16 says that "we have the mind of Christ [to be guided by His thoughts and purposes]." This means no matter what our circumstances may be, we can have God's wisdom, discernment, and peace to guide our decisions in the midst of them. I don't have to tell you that we live in an age full of dizzying distractions. It's amazing how much information is coming at us most of the time through technology, the media, and the busyness of the world around us.

This is the way of the world now, but we don't have

to live like the world. We can learn to reject the frustrations, distractions, and chaos of the world around us in order to have peace inside of us. It is this peace that will keep us focused and joyful no matter how crazy things around us may seem.

It was such a revelation for me when I realized I didn't have to think about just anything that came into my mind. I could choose my thoughts and do my own thinking—on purpose. And you can, too! There is a way to discover a new normal—a way to have victory in our circumstances and not live according to what the world views as normal. And it all begins with renewing our minds by focusing on God's promises rather than the world's problems. The choice is up to you.

So make the decision to rediscover your life by beginning to think a new way. Peaceful thoughts turn into a peaceful life! So start by spending time each day reading and meditating on the Word of God. Then pray and ask Him to help you understand how to apply the wisdom you discover to your everyday life. As you do your part to renew your mind, God will do His. You'll be amazed at how much better life can be when you have the mind of Christ. Don't be discouraged when you find you have gotten off track. Trust me when I say that it happens to all of us.

Allow God to Change You

Transformation needs to take place in our hearts first if we are going to see our lives transformed into ones we truly love. To be trans-formed means you are changed entirely from the inside out. Remember, when we become Christians we become new creations—"the

> *To be transformed means you are changed entirely from the inside out.*

old things [the previous moral and spiritual condition] have passed away. Behold, new things have come" (2 Corinthians 5:17).

If we will let Him, the Holy Spirit will work in us—changing our mind, will, and emotions—so we become more like Jesus day by day. As we grow spiritually, the good work that's happening inside us can be seen through the way we live, and we become testimonies of what God has done. We no longer have to go through life frustrated or bitter. We have discovered a better way to live!

Many people believe they can't change or be changed. They assume their lives are always going to be the same—never changing for the better. But the only thing that never changes is God (see Hebrews 13:8). And He wants us to dare to believe that He "is able to [carry out His purpose and] do superabundantly more than all that we dare ask or think [infinitely beyond our greatest prayers, hopes, or dreams]" (Ephesians 3:20). You may not realize it, but you are actually changing right now as you read the words in this book, because they are God's words and principles. You are learning new ways to think and your mind is being renewed. Keep reading, and if you need to, read it again and again.

Don't Forget…

- The Holy Spirit guides us so we can discover God's plan and purpose with each new day.
- We have two options: We can continue to be stressed-out until we fall apart, losing all of our peace and joy, or we can learn how to receive the peace Christ gives in every circumstance, rather than letting stress get into us.
- When we take time to renew our minds with God's Word, we learn how to think like God thinks, say what God says, and act like He wants us to act. This is the key to learning to love our lives!
- If we will let Him, the Holy Spirit will work in us—changing our mind, will, and emotions— so we become more like Jesus day by day.

No man is a failure who is enjoying life.

attributed to William Feather

CHAPTER 12

See Each Day as an Opportunity

One way to get the most out of life is to look upon it as an adventure.

William Feather

F. W. Woolworth was an incredibly successful businessman who pioneered the idea of the modern five-and-dime store. His business set trends and established what we now know as the highly successful model of low-priced retail. But it is his start in business that I find particularly interesting...

Some years ago, an energetic young man began as a clerk in a hardware store. Like many old-time hardware stores, the inventory included thousands of dollars' worth of items that were obsolete or seldom called for by customers.

The young man was smart enough to know that no thriving business could carry such an inventory and still show a healthy profit. He proposed a sale to get rid of the stuff. The owner was reluctant but finally agreed to let him set up a table in the middle of the store and try to sell a few of the oldest items.

Every product was priced at ten cents. The sale was a success and the young fellow got permission to run a second sale. It, too, went over just as well as the first. This gave the young clerk an idea. Why not open a store that would sell only nickel and dime items? He could run the store and his boss could supply the capital.

The young man's boss was not enthusiastic. "The plan will never work," he said, "because you can't find enough items to sell at a nickel and a dime." The young man was disappointed but eventually went ahead on his own and made a fortune out of the idea. His name was F. W. Woolworth.

Years later his old boss lamented, "As near as I can figure it, every word I used in turning Woolworth down has cost me about a million dollars!"[15]

F. W. Woolworth did something so few people choose to do: He seized his opportunity. He didn't wait for the perfect situation, he didn't complain when things were difficult, and he didn't stop when he met opposition. He looked for an opportunity and then he refused to give up on it.

I share that story with you because every new day in Christ is a new opportunity for something incredible to happen. Much like F. W. Woolworth,

all we have to do is boldly seize that daily opportunity. Look at what the Bible says in Psalm 84:11
(AMPC):

> For the Lord God is a Sun and Shield; the
> Lord bestows [present] grace and favor and
> [future] glory (honor, splendor, and heav-
> enly bliss)! No good thing will He withhold
> from those who walk uprightly.

That truth from the Word of God is so good you
should probably read it again. What an amazing
promise! The Lord "bestows

> Every new day in Christ
> is a new opportunity for
> something incredible to
> happen.

[present] grace and favor."
That means you have the
grace and favor of God *today*
to do something you could
not have done on your own. The grace and favor of
God are opening up opportunities for you...right
now...today!

And it gets even better. The verse goes on to say you
have that same grace and favor for "[future] glory."
There will be new opportunities from God tomorrow
and the next day and the next. Each new day with God
is a new opportunity to love your life!

You may read those words and think, *Well, I don't*

feel like my life is full of opportunity. I don't really see how each new day carries a new chance for something amazing to happen. I understand if you feel that way—sometimes we fail to see the opportunities we have. It's easy to get discouraged by past failures or distracted by present obstacles and overlook the opportunities just waiting to be seized. So let me give you five opportunities you have today that you may not have realized...

1. An Opportunity to Do Something You Have Been Afraid to Do Before

Fear is one of the main things that holds us back from living the abundant life Jesus came to give us—fear of the unknown, fear that we will fail, fear that we won't be good enough. But our lives in Christ no longer have to be lived in fear.

Isaiah 41:10 (AMPC) says, "Fear not [there is nothing to fear], for I am with you; do not look around you in terror and be dismayed, for I am your God... I will hold you up and retain you with My [victorious] right hand."

What an amazing opportunity! Today can be the day that you do something you've been afraid to do before. It can be the day you boldly and confidently face the challenges you've cowered from in the past. And you can do that because God promises that He will "hold you up and retain you" with His hand of victory.

- You may have been afraid to go back to get your degree...today is an opportunity to be courageous.
- You may have been afraid to apply for that job...today is an opportunity to be confident.
- You may have been afraid to be vulnerable again...today is an opportunity to be fearless.

Whatever fear has held you back, remember that 2 Timothy 1:7 says, "For God did not give us a spirit of timidity or cowardice or fear, but [He has given us a spirit] of power and of love and of sound judgment and personal discipline [abilities that result in a calm well-balanced mind and self-control]." Embrace your opportunity and do something courageous today in that spirit of power and love.

2. An Opportunity to Make Today Better Than Yesterday

Proverbs 4:18 tells us that "the path of the just (righteous) is like the light of dawn, that shines brighter and brighter until [it reaches its full strength and glory in] the perfect day."

God doesn't want you to live a stagnant life, repeating the same mistakes today that you made yesterday. Whatever mistakes you made yesterday...those are over. Whatever disappointment you may have faced yesterday...that day is in the rearview mirror. Today is a brand-new opportunity to start again. With God's help, you can determine to learn from the past and move forward. Today can be an amazing day!

3. An Opportunity to Pursue the Dream in Your Heart

Christopher Reeve said, "So many of our dreams... at first seem impossible. And then they seem improbable. And then when we summon the will, they soon become inevitable."[16]

The dream God gives you is much different from a wish or an aspiration. It is something that you can't get away from, something that seems to keep calling you forward. But unfortunately, many people don't pursue their dreams. They sit back idly, waiting for it to just happen on its own.

Whatever it is you feel like God is calling you to do, you will have to take active steps to pursue it. He will give you the strength you need, and He will make a way even when it seems impossible, but you have to step out in faith and move in the right direction. We all get where we want to go one step at a time, so make today a day when you take the opportunity to make more steps in the right direction.

There will never be a better time than now! Don't keep putting it off another day, another month, or another year. Be bold and realize today is your opportunity to get started. Do something, even if it's small, but refuse to do nothing. We can all pray today, and that should always be the first thing we do. If you have a dream, goal, or desire, and you don't know of anything you can do right now to work toward it, then pray and ask God to start opening doors.

4. An Opportunity to Do Something You Enjoy!

One of the things that will help us love our lives is regularly doing things that we enjoy. Although sacrificing for others is biblical and good, it is also good and emotionally healthy to do things that you enjoy. Last week I asked Dave to take me out for a coffee and he was glad to do it, but the coffee shop I wanted to go to required a one-hour round trip. I said, "It might seem foolish to take an hour driving to get a cup of coffee." But Dave said, "You are worth it." I not only appreciated his generous attitude, but I was reminded that we are all worth a little extravagance occasionally.

The coffee they serve is very good, and it comes out in a cute little cup and has perfect foam on top in the shape of a heart! My point is that I like it, and I took the opportunity to do something that I enjoy. You should do the same thing.

5. An Opportunity to Ask for Help

Have you ever been lost and thought, *I wish I had asked someone for directions*, or ever been struggling with a project on your own and thought, *I wish there was someone here who could help me?*

Help is something we all need from time to time but rarely ask for. Maybe we're too self-sufficient or too proud to admit we can't do it on our own; whatever the reason, we're frustrated in life because we just need help.

Well, I've got great news for you today: God is available to give you the direction you need and the help you require. Not only will God help you, but He will also provide other people to help you if you will ask Him to. I can honestly say that I don't know what I would do without all the people in my life who help me, but there was a time when I was so independent that I tried to do everything myself and would not ask for help. We all need each other, and we are actually robbing others of the opportunity to use the gifts God has given them if we refuse to let them help us.

- If you need wisdom for a decision, ask for help.
- If your body or soul is unhealthy, ask for help.
- If a relationship is in trouble, ask for help.
- If you need to make an attitude adjustment, ask for help.

Today is a great opportunity to invite God into your situation to turn things around. He has an amazing plan for your life and wants to see you walking in victory...all you have to do is ask for His help.

> Today is a great opportunity to invite God into your situation to turn things around.

Don't Wait—Go for It!

Your life in Christ is full of opportunities—you just have to look for them. Each new day is a new day to serve Him, experience His love, walk in the fullness of His joy, and love the life He came to give you. Don't waste another day sitting idly by, wishing you could catch a break. Take some initiative!

Don't Forget...

- You have the grace and favor of God *today* to do something you cannot do on your own.
- Today can be the day that you do something you've been afraid to do before.
- Today you can do something you enjoy!
- Today you can take one more step toward the fulfillment of your dreams.
- Today you can ask for help.

The purpose of life,
after all, is to live it, to
taste experience to the
utmost, to reach out
eagerly and without fear
for newer and richer
experience.

Eleanor Roosevelt

CHAPTER 13

The Five-Minute Rule

Worry often gives a small thing a big shadow.
Swedish proverb

We've all heard about the importance of time management. If you want to avoid stress, good time management is an effective way to do that. If you'll manage your calendar well, show up on time and work diligently to stay on task, your days will probably go much smoother. This is time management.

I think there is something just as important as time management—if not more—in order to live a life that you love. I like to call it "thought management." In order to love your life, it's wise to manage your thoughts with the same diligence you might manage your time. And a great way to do that is to live by The Five-Minute Rule.

The Five-Minute Rule is quite simple: *Don't spend even five minutes obsessing about something that won't matter five years, five months, or five weeks from now.* This is a practical tool that will help you love your life!

It's amazing to think of all the energy we expend thinking about things that don't matter. We obsess about the smallest things sometimes, not realizing that we are squandering our joy. We would be much wiser to focus our thoughts and our energy on the issues that really matter—the issues that will affect our lives in the long term.

Instead of obsessing over the irritations and minor issues in life, why not remind yourself that five days or less from now, they won't matter anyway?

Tormenting ourselves over issues (no matter *what* they are) never helps anything, and it certainly doesn't bring us peace and joy. It's a total waste of time. I'm reminded of the exasperated husband who asked his wife, "Why are you always worrying when it doesn't do any good?" She defensively responded, "Oh yes it does! Ninety percent of the things I worry about never happen."

I know a man who has a variety of OCD (Obsessive Compulsive Disorder) issues in his life. That means he has a compulsion to be obsessive about certain things. He cannot (or will not) be at peace and enjoy his life unless certain things are exactly the way he wants them to be. He is especially concerned about how everything in his life looks. His yard has to be manicured perfectly, his car has to be spotless, and if one of his children does anything that makes a smudge on it, he gets angry. His clothing and hair have to look a very specific way in order for him to be happy, but the truth is that the things that upset him are not even noticed by other people. His concern over these issues is very extreme when compared to the issues themselves. While we all have some things that are much more important to us than they might be to another person, anything carried to an extreme is an open door for the devil to torment us.

Philippians 4:6–7 says,

> Do not be anxious or worried about anything, but in everything [every circumstance and situation] by prayer and petition with thanksgiving, continue to make your [specific] requests known to God. And the peace of God [that peace which reassures the heart, that peace] which transcends all understanding, [that peace which] stands guard over your hearts and your minds in Christ Jesus [is yours].

And Matthew 6:25 says,

> Therefore I tell you, stop being worried or anxious (perpetually uneasy, distracted) about your life, as to what you will eat or

what you will drink; nor about your body, as
to what you will wear. Is life not more than
food, and the body more than clothing?

God's instructions are very clear here: Don't spend
any time obsessing about anything. Nothing in life
is perfect, and that is simply a fact that we all have to
deal with. On a practical level, here is what The Five-
Minute Rule might look like for you today . . .

- Don't spend even five minutes fuming over a
  traffic jam . . . it doesn't matter in the long run!
- Don't waste five minutes feeling insecure about
  what someone said about you . . . the only thing
  that really matters is what God says about you!
- Don't get angry for five minutes because you
  can't find the remote control or your cell
  phone . . . it will turn up!
- Don't lose your temper for five minutes when
  you don't get your way . . . God's way is best
  anyway!
- Don't spend five minutes panicking because
  your hair isn't cooperating today . . . it will look
  much better tomorrow!

Do you get the point? The Five-Minute Rule is all
about keeping your focus, and spending your energy,

on the things that really matter. Don't throw away your life five minutes at a time. Instead, ask God to give you a healthy sense of perspective so you can love your life every single day.

> The Five-Minute Rule is all about keeping your focus, and spending your energy, on the things that really matter.

Place Your Trust in God

Feeling worried or uneasy is a problem for so many in the world today. Of course, it's human nature to be concerned about the bad situations in our world and in our personal lives, but if we're not careful, the devil will cause us to worry beyond what's reasonable... beyond five minutes.

Keep in mind, worry is like a rocking chair—it's always in motion but it never gets you anywhere. This is why it is a total waste of time. And not only is it pointless, worry is dangerous because it steals our peace, physically wears us out, and can even make us sick.

Worry is the exact opposite of faith. When we worry, we're only tormenting ourselves, assuming the very worst. We're doing the devil's job for him when we stress-out over issues in our lives. There are very serious issues in life that require much more than five minutes of our time and thought, but they are limited compared to the number of things we let frustrate us that are not that important.

I was recently in a theater, and at the intermission of the show, Dave and I decided to move and sit with a friend a few rows behind us who was sitting in the aisle seat and had empty seats next to him. Because I thought I might need a restroom break before the end of the show, and since I didn't want to disturb anyone, I thought moving was a thoughtful choice. However, when I started to sit down the woman in the seat behind me became agitated and told me emphatically, "Do not sit in front of me!" She realized the seats were not our assigned seats, and she wanted to take pictures and didn't want me to sit there. I decided it was best to choose another seat and not cause a further disturbance, but I felt anger rising up in me. I had to apply The Five-Minute Rule, but I applied it in two minutes instead of five. I had a little chat with myself and told myself, *Joyce, you will probably never see this woman again in your life, and being angry won't change her, so drop it and go on enjoying your day.*

The only way to love your life is to not let things ruin your peace, and that is especially true with things that don't matter that much anyway. Peace doesn't just magically appear in our lives—we have to pursue it, crave it, and go after it!

Instead of focusing on all the minor things that are stealing your joy five minutes at a time, I have another suggestion. Follow the instruction found in Psalm 37:3 (AMPC). This Scripture gives us a great action step to overcoming fear, anxiety, and worry. It says:

> Trust (lean on, rely on, and be confident) in the Lord and do good; so shall you dwell in the land and feed surely on His faithfulness, and truly you shall be fed.

A Better Option

Rather than obsessing, worrying, and anxiously fretting your day away five minutes at a time, let me encourage you to do something much better. Give your mind to what you are doing at the moment. We miss a great deal of each day focused on things that have happened, instead of what is happening at the moment. Another option is to turn The Five-Minute Rule completely upside down and spend five minutes at a time engaging in faith-filled, positive thinking and activities that minister life to you, rather than misery.

- Spend five consecutive minutes thanking God for all His blessings.

- Take five minutes to help someone around you today.
- Go to God and spend five minutes in prayer the next time you feel overwhelmed by the events of your day.
- Call and encourage a friend for five minutes.
- Declare promises from the Bible over your life for five minutes before you go to bed.

It's all about perspective. If you'll do things in intervals (even as short as five minutes) that have real, lasting, eternal impact, you're going to find your attitude and outlook on life becoming so much better. You'll start to love your life … five minutes at a time!

Don't Forget …

- In order to enjoy the life Jesus came to give you, it's wise to manage your thoughts with the same diligence with which you manage your time.
- Focus your thoughts and energy on the issues that really matter—the issues that will affect your life in the long term.
- The Five-Minute Rule is quite simple: *Don't spend even five minutes obsessing about something that won't matter five years, five months, or five weeks from now.*

- Worry is like a rocking chair—it keeps you busy, but it never gets you anywhere.
- Don't throw away your life five minutes at a time. Instead, ask God to give you a healthy sense of perspective so you can love your life every single day.

Cherish your yesterdays,
dream your tomorrows,
and live your todays.

Anonymous

CHAPTER 14

Live Every Day Like It's Your Last

It is not the years in your life but the life in your years that counts.

Adlai Stevenson

I believe you are well on your way to truly living a life that you love. But before we go any further, there is something else we need to discuss…and it may be the most important thing of all: One of the best ways to live a life you love is to live every day like it's your last. Start doing the things that are important to you, and things that you enjoy.

I'm not talking about living in fear that today could be your last day on Earth; I'm encouraging you to make the most of each day. I don't know about you, but one of the things that can frustrate me is wasting time. I am goal-oriented and I like to accomplish something, even if it is something small, each day. When we think we have endless days left, we may tend to procrastinate when it comes to doing things that we want to do, but it is very unwise to do that.

You may have seen the movie *The Bucket List*, in which two men who were terminally ill each made a list of things they had always wanted to do but had never done. Realizing their time was coming to an end, they made a decision to get busy doing the things that they should have been doing throughout their lives. I know of several people who made their own bucket lists after seeing that movie, and they got more serious about taking time to do some of the things in life that they really wanted to do.

None of us can spend our days just doing things we want to do. We all have responsibilities that need to come first, but if we do not add things that we enjoy, life can become very bland very quickly. I look at it like adding some salt, pepper, or other spice to my food. The spice is not everything, but it sure helps the flavor. Adding some spice to your life doesn't mean that you have to do something big that requires a lot of time and money. Instead of finding reasons why you can't do a thing, why not find ways that you can? Or, if you cannot do exactly what you want to do, then do some version of it. If you would love to travel through Europe but that is impossible right now, then at least go somewhere that you have never been.

Now, if you don't have the finances to do some of the things you would like to do, then it's necessary to put them off until another time. There are plenty of reasons why we need to wait on doing some things, but we don't have to wait to do everything we enjoy. Make your own list. What are several things you want to do before your time on Earth is over? Once you know what you want to do, try to schedule at least some of them every year. Have things on your list that are big and some that are little, so you always have a variety to choose from.

Don't be the kind of person who watches other people do things and then says, "I've always wanted to do that, but I guess I will never get to." When we do that, we are likely to feel deprived and then end up resenting the life we have instead of loving it. If you cannot do the things you would like to do now, at least you can say, "Someday I am going to do that!" Hope energizes us and gives us something to look forward to.

Enjoyment

I recall being astounded at one time many years ago when I realized through studying Scripture that Jesus came so that we might have and enjoy our lives (see John 10:10).

My son and his wife just took a weekend and went to a nice local hotel. They have three small children and wanted a break from the routine of everyday life. They ate out, did some shopping, and had an opportunity to talk with one another without being continually interrupted by young children, who ask a question every few minutes. I was very happy for them, and their joy and enjoyment gave me enjoyment. Jesus feels the same way about us—our enjoyment gives Him joy!

Part of enjoyment is laughter, and it is more than a good idea—it's a biblical one! God gave us the capacity to laugh, and we would be wise to make the most of it. Laughter brings health to the soul...and the body. Over the years I've read and heard so much about the benefits of laughter. For example, it is common knowledge that laughter can improve your health in the following ways:

- Laughter causes the release of endorphins, a chemical in the body that relieves pain and creates a sense of well-being.
- Laughter can raise your energy level, relieve tension, and change your attitude.
- Laughter is generally known to increase antibodies and strengthen your immune system.

- A hearty belly laugh causes you to inhale more oxygen and stimulates your heart and blood circulation. It's like internal aerobic exercise!

I have found that the things that make me laugh the most are not expensive. They usually happen when I am not trying to entertain myself but am just living my ordinary, daily life. I love to spend time with people who have a good sense of humor and tend to make me laugh a lot. Time spent with them is very refreshing to me. Like most of you, I work very hard and could easily get so focused on my responsibilities that I don't take the time for laughter, but it is important in more ways than we might think.

Thankfully I have some people in my immediate family that are blessed with a quick wit and I am thankful for that. I believe that the ability to make other people laugh is a gift from God.

One of the ways to laugh more is to be less serious about some things. Although there are many very serious issues in life that we deal with, there are other things we get intense about when we really don't need to. The mistakes we make in life is one of those things. Learn to laugh at yourself instead of berating yourself for your imperfections.

Children find a way to laugh no matter what, and

we can learn a lot from them. Become more childlike and make a decision to laugh more and worry less.

Celebrate!

In addition to doing things that you want to do, I also want to encourage you to begin to celebrate. You don't need to wait for some major accomplishment in life, like graduating from college or getting married, to celebrate. You can and should begin to celebrate small victories in your life. Celebration doesn't need to be expensive, and it is something you can do by yourself. It is more about an attitude than it is an event.

In order to live a life that you love, you will need to stop keeping a running inventory of all the things you think are wrong with yourself and your life. We have a very strong tendency as humans to focus on how far we have to go instead of how far we have come, and on what we don't have instead of what we do have. This Scripture has really helped me overcome these tendencies:

> What the eyes see [enjoying what is available] is better than [craving] what the soul desires. This too is futility and chasing after the wind.
>
> Ecclesiastes 6:9

Solomon, the writer of Ecclesiastes, was a man who made it a priority to learn how to enjoy life. Although he tried many things that utterly failed—one of which was living for himself alone—he did come to some conclusions that I agree with. One of those is summed up in this Scripture. It simply says it is much better to enjoy what we have than it is to continually crave what we don't have.

Have you ever met one of those people who is *never* satisfied, no matter what is going on in their life? I have, and it can be exhausting just being with them. Although they may even say that they are blessed, their list of complaints is so long that their blessings get lost in it. They focus on the negatives in life instead of the positive things. They think they will be happy "when" and "if," but somehow, they never get around to enjoying where they are and what they have *now*.

If we were to live every day like it was our last, I seriously doubt that we would continue to put off enjoyment. We all seem to inherently know that it is important, but we assign it to some day in the future. "Now" is what we have, so let's start making the best use of it that we can.

I have been in a season of God dealing with me about some of my faults and weaknesses, and I found myself dwelling on them too much recently. I had to stop and remember how far I have come in spiritual growth instead of just how far I still have to go. When God shows us our flaws, it is not so we can dwell on them and become discouraged; it is an act of His love for us and His way of helping us improve. If you will let Him, He will also show you how far you have come in your journey with Him. Celebrate those successes regularly, and it will help you deal more effectively with the things that still need to change.

When God calls me home and the people who love me get together to remember my life, I don't want them to be sad and miserable—I want them to celebrate my memory and accomplishments. God wants us to do that every day! Enjoy today and live it as if it might be your last.

Make Up Your Mind to Love Your Life Today

Louis E. Boone said, "The saddest summary of a life contains three descriptions: could have, might have, and should have."[17] And I think he's right. There are so many people living a could-have, might-have, should-have kind of life. But that doesn't have to be you. You can live today like it's your last day on Earth, maximizing every moment. Be sure that you let the people you love know how you feel. Don't wait until it's too late and then live with regret over things that you intended to tell them, but just never did. Instead of *could have, might have,* or *should have,* you can live a life of *I loved! I laughed! I lived fully!*

Don't Forget...

- Live every day as if it were your last.
- Start doing the things you have always wanted to do.
- Celebrate every little victory in your life.
- Tell people how important they are to you.
- Enjoy life now and don't let anything stop you.

Well, your greatest joy
definitely comes from
doing something for
another, especially when
it was done with no
thought of something in
return.

John Wooden

CHAPTER 15

Be the You God Created You to Be

What lies behind us and what lies before us are tiny matters compared to what lies within us.
attributed to Ralph Waldo Emerson

One of the best ways to love your life is choosing to be comfortable with yourself. Until you do that, your attitude, your relationships, and your own peace of mind will be greatly compromised. Being the you God created you to be is of the utmost importance... and it only makes sense. Let me show you what I mean...

My friend Darlene Zschech is one of the most gifted singers and worship leaders I have ever met. When she stands up to lead worship, it really is incredible to watch. This is her gifting—she's great at it. But can you imagine if all of a sudden, Darlene decided she wanted to be a race-car driver? Maybe she saw a race on TV and decided, *It would be so cool if only I could drive that fast.* I don't suspect it would go very well. I would be afraid for her safety. Why? Because Darlene wasn't created to drive race cars.

I have another great friend, Christine Caine, who is incredibly gifted to teach the Word of God. That's who God made her to be. But what if Chris decided one day that she wanted to be a Hollywood movie star? As talented as she is, she's never told me that acting is her desire or dream in life. And if she tried to find happiness by starring in the next big-budget summer movie, she would probably end up very frustrated.

Darlene and Christine would be the first to tell you that they are happiest when they are operating with their unique skill sets...not trying to be someone else.

I can relate to this idea because it took me quite a while to learn to be comfortable being myself. I've tried to be a number of different things over the years that just weren't me. I remember when I tried to learn the guitar; it did not go well. I also remember when I decided I was going to be a homemaker who baked for my family all day and sewed new outfits for all of us to wear. Wow...what a mistake. I'd never been so frustrated in my life.

No matter how hard I tried, these things just weren't me. And guess what? The more frustrated I became trying to be like other people, the more my relationships suffered. I had so much more peace (and the people around me felt the same way) when I realized God had created me to teach His Word and *that* was going to be my focus.

But it wasn't only my skills that I compared with other people; I also compared my temperament and personality to others'. I am aggressive, straightforward, and bold, but as I watched other women who were quieter and sweeter in nature, I let the devil convince me that something was wrong with me and that I needed to be more like they were. I did need to go through some changes. I needed to improve in the way I presented myself to other people. I was a bit harsh due to abuse I had experienced. Over the years, God has softened my heart and given me more wisdom in how I function in relationships, but I still had to learn to embrace the temperament and personality that God created me to have. And so do you!

What about you? Are you content with the person God created you to be, or are you constantly trying to be like someone else? If you've ever thought, *I've got nothing to offer,* or *I wish I could be like so-and-so,* God wants to set you free from that. God created you to be a unique individual; He

> God wants you to be comfortable being yourself.

assigned your talents and abilities, and He wants you to be comfortable being yourself. That doesn't mean you never try new things, and it doesn't mean other people can't inspire you to branch out and learn something different; it simply means you realize you are amazing and talented just the way God created you—you don't have to be like someone else!

Psalm 139:13 says:

> For You formed my innermost parts; You knit me [together] in my mother's womb.

And verse 14 goes on to say:

> I will give thanks and praise to You, for I am fearfully and wonderfully made; wonderful are Your works, and my soul knows it very well.

These verses tell you that God took careful time in creating you. He knew exactly what He was doing when He meticulously designed your spirit, soul, and body. He has given you unique talents, a beautiful personality, and an individual purpose. Get excited—you can celebrate the person God has created you to be!

Overcoming Insecurity

Many people in the world today are dealing with an identity crisis. It happens because they don't really understand who they are in Christ. God wants us to find our worth and value in the fact that we were created by Him, we belong to Him, He loves us, and He has a very good plan for our lives. But instead of finding their identity in Him, many base their worth and value on other things—what they look like, what career they have, who they know, or what they own. But none of these things define who God has created you to be.

If you've ever dealt with insecurity, relax—you're normal. We all have! But the good news is we don't have to *stay* insecure. We don't have to live unhappily, stuck in our lack of confidence. We were created to feel safe, secure, confident, and bold—this is part of our spiritual DNA as God's children. But the key to living that secure life in Christ is knowing who you were created to be, really receiving God's unconditional love for you, and basing your worth on what the Word of God says about you, rather than anything else.

Isaiah 54:17 says: "This [peace, righteousness, *security*, and triumph over opposition] is the heritage of the servants of the Lord" (emphasis added). I love this verse of Scripture, because it clearly shows us that it is our inherited right through our relationship with Christ to be secure. We don't have to go through life wishing we were someone else or wondering what others think about us—we can be safe and secure and free to be the unique person God created us to be.

Think about this: The Word of God tells us that we are joint heirs with Jesus (see Romans 8:17) and whatever He has, we inherit as a gift from Him. Isn't that incredible? But in order to live in the reality of that truth, we have to receive it by faith, and that requires that we believe it before we receive it.

- You may not always feel talented ... but you are!
- You may not think you are important ... but you are!
- You may not see that you are blessed ... but you are!
- You may not think you are loved ... but you are!

We base our faith on the truth of God's Word, and that kind of faith always declares (talks about) what it believes even before it is seen or manifested. Speaking your faith helps renew your mind, and it actually increases your faith. What we believe about ourselves is greatly affected by our thoughts and words. I encourage you to speak what the Bible says about you. God not only sees what we are at this moment, but He sees what we are becoming. He sees the end from the beginning (see Isaiah 46:10). This will help you overcome any negative beliefs you have and will enable you to defeat the evil opposition that wants to steal your destiny, your peace and joy.

God Loves You More Than You Can Imagine

Karl Barth was one of the greatest theologians of the twentieth century. He was brilliant and wrote extensively about theology, faith, and culture. Toward the end of his life, he was giving a lecture at the University of Chicago Divinity School. As you can imagine, the lecture hall was packed. After the lecture was over, an eager student asked Barth what he considered to be the greatest theological discovery of his life.

Everyone in attendance that day sat on the edge of their seat, waiting to hear what this brilliant theologian would say, what profound truth he would unveil. Karl Barth thought for a moment, then smiled and answered, "The greatest theological insight that I have ever had is this: Jesus loves me, this I know, for the Bible tells me so."[18]

I think it is amazing that a children's Sunday school song can effectively sum up the very basis of our salvation—God loves us more than we can imagine. If only more people understood the depth of this powerful message.

For years, I was one of those people who didn't quite understand God's love for me. It was a truth that I needed revelation about early in my ministry. In fact, the first message I ever preached was about God's love for us.

I remember that I didn't particularly want to preach on that topic, because I felt like it wasn't new information or especially exciting—I assumed people already knew that God loved them. But the Lord impressed on my heart that many people didn't understand His love, and if they did, they would live much differently. We wouldn't compare ourselves with others, get caught up in competition, or be afraid of admitting weaknesses if we were truly secure in God's love.

First John 4:18 (AMPC) says:

> There is no fear in love [dread does not exist], but full-grown (complete, perfect) love turns fear out of doors and expels every trace of terror!

As I studied this verse, I began to realize I was a person who had yet to understand the "full-grown (complete, perfect)" love of the Father. I still had fear, insecurity, and doubts about whether I deserved His love. So for the next year of my life, I studied the love of God, and during that time of study, I began to get a personal revelation of God's unconditional love and acceptance of me . . . and for all those who call on His name. I find that we often try to exist on information alone, but what we truly need is revelation. We need revelation about the love that God has for us and to be rooted deeply in it.

> May Christ through your faith [actually] dwell (settle down, abide, make His permanent home) in your hearts! May you be rooted deep in love and founded securely on love.
>
> Ephesians 3:17 (AMPC)

It was this revelation of God's unconditional love that helped me understand that my worth and value are found in the truth that I am a child of God, not in what I do, what I have, what I look like, or what others think about me. Of course, we all want to look our best, do great things, and be well thought of, but if we are secure in God's love and we don't happen to achieve those things, we can still hold our head high and believe we are loved and valuable. When we do that, we're putting our faith in God to be in charge of our lives, rather than our circumstances.

No matter what career you have, how much money you do or don't have, whether you're single or married, or you have children or not, you are valued, accepted, and loved unconditionally by your Heavenly Father.

This is so important to understand, because if you falsely believe the love of God is based on what you do for a living or how well you perform in your daily life, you will never be truly secure and stable in your relationship with Him. But when you grasp that God loves you unconditionally, simply for who you are, you will be free to love your life and enjoy the person He has created you to be.

Three Ways to Be the You God Created You to Be

When you like yourself, it is so much easier to enjoy your life. And here is a side benefit: When you learn to accept and get along with yourself, you tend to have better relationships; you can better accept and get along with others.

The Bible tells us on multiple occasions to love your neighbor as yourself. For many people who have a difficult time getting along with others, the actual root of the problem is a difficulty to believe in their own self-worth.

Matthew 7:17 says: "Even so, every healthy tree bears good fruit, but the unhealthy tree bears bad fruit." That means that the "fruit" of our lives comes from the "root" within us. If you have roots of inferiority, shame, rejection, or self-loathing in your soul, the fruit of your relationships will suffer. But once you get a revelation of God's unconditional love for you and begin to accept the person He created you to be, this new root will produce great fruit and your relationships will bloom beautifully. I would like to recommend that you search your heart and honestly ask yourself if you truly believe beyond a shadow of a doubt that God loves you at all times, whether you are behaving perfectly or not. Until you can answer a definite yes to that question, then you need to continue studying and meditating on Scriptures about the love that God has for you, and eventually, it will become a revelation that no one or nothing can ever take away from you. Paul encourages us to never let anything—not trouble, persecution, things threatening or impending or anything else in all the world—to separate us from God's love (see Romans 8:35, 38–39).

Here are three practical ways to establish healthy spiritual roots that will transform your outlook on life:

1. Speak good things about yourself that God speaks...never bad.

Matthew 12:37 says, "For by your words you will be acquitted, and by your words you will be condemned" (NIV). Proverbs 23:7 says as a man "thinks in his heart, so is he" (NKJV). These verses give us a very powerful truth we need to understand: The way we talk and think about ourselves reveals how we feel about ourselves.

So let me suggest you start changing your attitude about yourself by changing the way you talk about yourself. Never say things like, *I look terrible. I'm stupid. Who could ever love me? I never do anything right.* These negative words only reinforce a root of insecurity. Instead, begin saying things that are in line with what the Word of God says about you. Things like...

- I am more than a conqueror through Him Who loves me (Romans 8:37).
- I am God's workmanship (Ephesians 2:10).
- I am the righteousness of God in Christ Jesus (2 Corinthians 5:21).
- I am greatly loved by God (1 John 4:10).

This is so easy to do! You can make these declarations while you're making dinner, while you're sitting in traffic, or when you first get up in the morning. You'll be amazed at how speaking God's truth about who you really are will change your perspective and greatly benefit your relationships.

2. Focus on your potential, not your limitations.

Great athletes never focus on the last shot they missed, the previous catch they dropped, or last inning's strikeout; instead, they anxiously await their next opportunity to make an incredible play. I'm not much of a sports fan, but I can appreciate this mindset. One of the things that makes them champions is their decision to focus on their ability to do better next time, rather than their mistakes and failures. The athlete, or any successful person, is focusing on their potential rather than their limitations. We would be wise to do the same thing!

Instead of obsessing about what you can't do, start praising God for the things you can do. Maximize your strengths and minimize your weaknesses. God gave you those talents, that personality, or those interests, for a reason. Ask Him to help you see how you can make the most of the beautiful, unique talents and abilities He has given you.

3. *Stand out from the crowd… don't be like everyone else.*

God obviously loves variety because He created us all differently, even down to our unique fingerprints. You'll never love your life if you're spending that life trying to be like other people. There will always be people in your life who are great examples to follow, but don't lose your own identity by trying to be just like them. Allow your own unique personality traits to distinguish you from the rest of the crowd. God created you to be different—embrace the beauty of that truth.

If everything is the same, then nothing stands out and shines. It is God's infinite variety combined together that creates amazing beauty. When I walk outside, I notice the endless variety of trees, plants, flowers, grasses, and even weeds. They are all special and unique, and through working together with all the others, they create a beautiful world we can be amazed by. If everything was exactly alike, nothing would stand out, and I might not notice anything.

If you'll apply these three practical instructions to your life, I'm confident it will help strengthen both your self-image and your personal relationships. Remember, there is only one you, so go out and enjoy the beautiful, talented, unique you God created you to be!

Don't Forget...

- One of the best ways to love your life is choosing to be comfortable being yourself.
- You don't have to be like someone else to be happy.
- God knew exactly what He was doing when He meticulously designed your spirit, soul, and body. He has given you unique talents, a beautiful personality, and an individual purpose.
- We were created to feel safe, secure, confident, and bold—this is part of our spiritual DNA as born-again believers.
- You are valued, accepted, and loved unconditionally by your Heavenly Father.

God cannot give us
happiness and peace
apart from Himself,
because it is not there.
There is no such thing.

C. S. Lewis

SECTION III

Love Other People and You Will Love Your Life

I am giving you a new commandment, that you love one another. Just as I have loved you, so you too are to love one another.

John 13:34

CHAPTER 16

The Power of Love

Love is what makes the ride worthwhile.
attributed to Franklin P. Jones

You can't live a life that you love unless love is the central theme of your life. This is the number one premise of this book. It's only when love is your primary pursuit that you begin to have purpose and truly enjoy your life on a regular basis.

I say this because love is the most powerful force in the world. The Bible tells us that God is love. So when you make love the focus of your life, you're making God the number one priority in your life. First John 4:8 tells us very plainly: "The one who does not love has not become acquainted with God [does not and never did know Him], for God is love." If you want to be acquainted with God, it is essential that you live a life of unconditional love.

Now, I'm not talking about a romantic love or an emotional love that only acts on feelings of exhilaration. I'm talking about a *decision* to love—loving God because He first loved you, loving yourself because you are made in God's image, and loving others even when you don't particularly feel like it. This is real love, what the Bible calls agape love. This is a love with no strings attached.

Anybody can love people who treat them well. It takes no effort to love a coworker who has never said a bad word about you. It's quite easy to love a neighbor who keeps a perfect yard and never gets on your nerves. This isn't love so much as it is appreciation— *You're nice to me, so I'll be nice to you in return.* But what about that person who offended you? How about the family member who is frustrating and gets on your nerves? How do you handle the person who started that rumor about your family? Is love the central theme of your life when it comes to these people?

I learned a long time ago that I can't control the actions of other people. I can't make them act a certain way or treat me the way I'd like to be treated. The simple fact is there are always going to be people who hurt our feelings, overlook our needs, or fail to show kindness and sympathy. But even though I can't control how they act toward me, there is one thing I can control…

I can control how I respond to them!

I can show love in the face of opposition. I can display generosity even if they have been selfish around me. I can pay a compliment, share an encouragement, or offer a prayer . . . even when I don't feel they deserve it. And you know what? You can, too! You can live a life of love, regardless of the actions or behaviors of those around you.

When we choose to focus on what we can do—demonstrate love every day—instead of what others are doing, an amazing thing begins to happen. Rather than being discouraged and upset because of what someone else has said or done, we are filled with joy because love is our priority. The more we love others, the happier and more fulfilled we become. Loving others is the primary ingredient to living a life that we love!

> *Loving others is the primary ingredient to living a life that we love!*

The Joy of Learning to Love

Love, like everything else in life, is something we must learn to do. While it is natural to easily love your own children or a devoted spouse, loving others isn't always so easy. It takes practice and determination—it is a learned behavior.

Learning is a natural part of life. Each new day brings exciting new opportunities to learn something we didn't know before. As long as we are willing and open to receive, God will always teach us things that will be a benefit to us and to others.

I've been studying and teaching the Word of God for many years now, but I'm still learning... and I'm happy to know that I always will be. As the old saying goes, God isn't finished with me yet! And the things God continues to show me about love enrich my life in deep ways. I'm at a place in my life where I can honestly say, "Lord, eliminate everything in my life that's holding me back. Please take away anything that's keeping me from walking in love and finding true fulfillment in my life."

I hope you will be able to say the same thing, because I know how profoundly it will change your life. When we can say, "Lord, teach me the joy of living a life of love," our entire perspective of life shifts. It's like someone turns on the light in a dark room. We begin to see things we could never see before. Love always drives away the darkness from our lives.

Here are three components to living a life of love.

1. Loving God

This is the most important aspect of love—receiving God's love and then loving Him in return. Deuteronomy 6:5 says, "You shall love the Lord your God with all your heart and mind and with all your soul and with all your strength [your entire being]." Jesus repeats this instruction in the New Testament and even says it is the most important commandment (along with loving your neighbor as yourself... more about this in a moment).

People often ask me, "But how do I love God? Is it by telling Him? By going to church? By singing praises?" These are all good things, but they are just the beginning. We show God our love through our obedience to Him. After all, actions speak louder than words. Jesus said it very plainly in John 14:15, "If you [really] love Me, you will keep and obey My commandments."

I've discovered that our level of obedience grows as we get to know and experience God's love, His goodness, and His faithfulness in our lives. Our desire to follow and obey the Lord's commandments will increase as we increase our love for Him.

2. Loving Yourself

Sometimes when people hear the phrase "loving yourself," they think it sounds selfish. *Why would I love myself? I don't want to be self-focused.* But there is something important that people often fail to realize: You

> You cannot give away something you don't have in you.

cannot give away something you don't have in you. How can someone love another person if they don't love themselves?

When Jesus talked about the greatest commandment, He quoted Deuteronomy 6:5, saying that we are to love God with all of our heart, but He also said: "You shall [unselfishly] love your neighbor as yourself" (Mark 12:31). Isn't that incredible? Even though you know your faults and flaws, even though you know you're not perfect, even though you may disappoint yourself from time to time, Jesus wants you to learn to love yourself!

Let me encourage you to accept yourself and embrace your personality, and even your imperfections. Become your own best ally and friend. You may not yet be where you want to be, but you're making progress. Jesus died for you because you have weaknesses and imperfections, so don't reject yourself because of them. God wants you to love yourself and to keep working to make progress in becoming the person He has created you to be.

3. Loving Others

While we often think of loving others (especially difficult people) as something that is tremendously hard to do, I have good news for you: It's easier than you think! When you first learn to love God and then learn to love yourself, loving others is a natural by-product. It will happen more easily than you ever thought possible. As a matter of fact, showing love to other people will become a complete joy! I know from Scripture (see Romans 12:21) that we overcome evil with good. I believe this is a great spiritual secret, and when we do it, it adds tremendous spiritual power to our lives. If we can be good and kind to the people who are mean and unkind to us, then we can do just about anything else that we need to do in life. Jesus did it, and when we do it, then we are like Him.

First John 3:14 says: "We know that we have passed over out of death into Life, because we love the brothers and sisters." "Life" in this verse is referring to the life of God, or life as God has it.

The key to living the best life God has for you is to love others. It is the only way to keep the life of God Himself flowing through you. God's love is a gift to us—it is in us—but we need to release that love to other people through our words and actions. If we don't release the love of God that is in us, it will become stagnant, like a pool of water with no outlet.

> The key to living the best life God has for you is to love others.

I have to tell you, the simple act of loving others is

one of the most enjoyable things I have experienced. When I plan to do something to bless someone else, I get excited! It brings me so much joy!

You can experience that same exhilaration. Let me give you a challenge: Think of two or three people you know who could really use a gesture of love and kindness today. Now think of some creative ways you can express the love of God to these people. When you put your plan into action, I guarantee you will feel a sense of complete joy and fulfillment afterward.

Loving God, loving yourself, loving others—if you will dedicate yourself to loving in these three areas, you'll be amazed at the difference it makes.

More Than Talk

Russell Herman was a sixty-seven-year-old carpenter who died in 1994. What really sets him apart was the incredible set of bequests he left behind—more than two billion dollars for East St. Louis, another billion and a half for the State of Illinois, two and a half billion for the national forest system, and a very impressive six trillion dollars to the government to help pay off the national debt. Wow! That's some incredible generosity!

But there was a small problem—when he died, Herman's only real asset was a 1983 Oldsmobile.

No millions, no billions, and certainly no trillions. Herman made incredible promises, and some very grand announcements, but there wasn't any real generosity because he couldn't actually back up his pronouncements.[19]

When I think about this story of Russell Herman, I'm reminded that love is more than words—love is action. It doesn't matter how much we talk about blessing others or even how many times we say the words, "I love you." Those are just empty promises if we aren't actively demonstrating love in real, noticeable, tangible ways. C. S. Lewis said, "Do not waste your time bothering whether you 'love' your neighbor; act as if you did. As soon as we do this, we find one of the great secrets. When you are behaving as if you loved someone, you will presently come to love him."[20] Action is the key!

> Love is more than words—love is action.

I'm reminded that the apostle Paul told us in James 2:14: "What is the benefit, my fellow believers, if someone claims to have faith but has no [good] works [as evidence]?" And he went on to bluntly say that faith without works is dead (see James 2:17). I think the same is true for love. What good is it for anyone to profess to have love if he has no good works to show it? If we really want to live a life of love, it is important that we look for ways to actively demonstrate that life.

The good news is—that's the enjoyable part! Demonstrating kindness, sharing happiness, giving love—these are the things that can turn around any bad mood and help us really enjoy life. So let me encourage you today to:

- Surprise a neighbor with a homemade dessert, or cut their grass while you are cutting yours.
- Take your spouse out for a nice dinner and let them know how much you appreciate their hard work.
- Ask a coworker out for coffee and inquire about their life.
- Send your child's or grandchild's teacher a note of encouragement, telling them what a great job they're doing.
- Volunteer to babysit so some friends can go out to dinner.

There are countless ways to show love to the people in your life, so start taking advantage of those opportunities today. Be creative—in big or small, simple or elaborate ways—when you take action steps to love others. It will do more than just bless them... it will bless you, too! It's one of the best things you can do to really enjoy your life. So don't wait another moment—get started today!

Don't Forget...

- You can't live a life that you love unless love is the central theme of your life.
- The most important aspect of love is receiving God's love and then loving Him in return.
- Accept yourself and embrace your personality, and even your imperfections. You may not yet be where you want to be, but you're making progress. Enjoy where you are on the way to where you're going!
- God's love is a gift to us—it is in us—but we need to release that love to other people through our words and actions.
- If we really want to live a life of love, it is important that we look for ways to actively demonstrate that love.

[The Christian] does not think God will love us because we are good, but that God will make us good because He loves us.

C. S. Lewis

CHAPTER 17

Build the Right Environment

My best friend is the one who brings out the best in me.

attributed to Henry Ford

Have you ever had a fish tank? Or have you ever known someone who has a fish tank? I ask because I have a friend who is a fish enthusiast—he loves his fish tank! But I'm not talking about a small, one-gallon fish bowl that sits on top of his desk. The smallest tank he's ever had is a fifty-five-gallon tank.

Hearing him talk about the time invested in caring for his fish and maintaining his fish tank is very interesting. I suppose a lot of people assume you can just dump some water in the tank and then purchase a few fish and you're on your way. But that's not how it works. To have a successful tank, and to keep the fish alive, you have to go to great lengths to develop the right environment. You have to have the correct size filters, maintain proper chemical balances in the water, put only certain types of fish together, use the correct type and amount of food...there is quite a lot to it!

I'm not sure I'm cut out to be a fish enthusiast, but I know many people who are. Whether it's a saltwater or freshwater tank, they love building the right environment in order to enjoy healthy fish.

You know, I think our lives have some similarities to those fish tanks, because in order to stay healthy (in our spirit, soul, and body) it is important that we develop a safe, clean, supportive environment around us. You're never going to love your life if you are swimming in dirty water. That's why it is essential that you build the right environment for your life.

What you surround yourself with matters. If you fill your life with distractions, negativity, poor influences, and dysfunctional relationships, it is going to be impossible to enjoy any part of your day. Instead, you are going to succumb to the unhealthy environment and become unhealthy yourself. This is not what God wants for your life. He wants to see you flourish and thrive. If you'll let Him, He will help you surround yourself with encouraging, life-giving influences that will bring joy and happiness every day of your life.

I could probably write an entire book on how to build the right environment for your life and how to surround yourself with godly influences, but there are three things I want to focus on in this chapter.

Build Your Life on the Word of God

If you have heard me speak or read any of my books, you already know that I am a firm believer in the power of God's Word. We are taught in Scripture that if we build our house on the rock, it will stand through any storm in life (see Matthew 7:24–27).

There is no better influence for your life than the Word of God—it is filled with His promises, instructions, and assurances of love for you. Making the Bible the central foundation of your life is the most important thing you can do. I can say without hesitation that if you want to love your life, then you will need to love God's Word.

> If you want to love your life, then you will need to love God's Word.

Jeremiah 15:16 says:

> Your words were found and I ate them, and
> Your words became a joy to me and the
> delight of my heart; for I have been called by
> Your name, O Lord God of hosts.

The prophet Jeremiah says it plainly. He found joy and delight in filling himself with the Word of God!

Psalm 19:8 says:

> The precepts of the Lord are right, bringing
> joy to the heart; the commandment of the
> Lord is pure, enlightening the eyes.

The psalmist David said that we are "blessed
(happy, fortunate, to be envied)" when we walk and
order our conduct according to the Word of God (see
Psalm 119:1 AMPC).

There are many biblical references that connect joy
with the study of God's Word. I know for sure that I
was not enjoying or loving my life prior to becoming
a student of God's Word. Studying God's Word may
seem like a daunting task, but if you will just begin
and keep it up day after day, you will see for yourself
what a difference it can make. You don't have to study
for hours each day, but if you dedicate some time to
it and do it regularly, eventually you will be surprised
by how much you know and how it has changed your
life for the better.

I've spent more than forty years studying God's
Word, and it has totally changed my life. I've learned
so much, but it didn't happen right away. It took a
conscious decision to surround myself with the Word.
If you want to see areas of your life change, learn to
truly study the Bible and you'll be amazed at what it

will do in your family, your finances, your relationships, your emotions...every part of who you are.

The Bible is the best-selling book in history, but it
is no ordinary book. The words within its pages are
life to your soul. Proverbs 4:20–22 (AMPC) says it this
way:

> My son, attend to my words; consent and
> submit to my sayings. Let them not depart
> from your sight; keep them in the center of
> your heart. For they are life to those who
> find them, healing and health to all their
> flesh.

The Bible is God's Word given directly to you!
And when you build your life around God's Word,
you will begin to see changes that only His truth can
bring. The good news is, it won't take you thirty years
to know what you need to know. Just begin where
you are right now and determine to keep going. Every
time you study the Bible and pay attention to what
you're reading, your life is being changed.

The word "attend" in the Scripture mentioned
above (Proverbs 4:20–22) means "to pay attention
to," to "give some time" to something. To attend to
the Word of God means more than just reading it; it
means you meditate on the Word. You let the words

on the pages soak into your spirit. You don't have to rush through a daily reading plan. It is not important to check off some sort of spiritual to-do list, thinking, *Okay, today I read X number of chapters or X number of words—I did my spiritual duty.* No, the best way to build your life around the Bible is to sit down and ask the Lord to show you something today through His Word. After reading for a little while, look back over what you have read and jot down a few things you saw that interested you or that you learned. It is amazing how many different lessons there are in just one chapter of the Bible.

If you could buy "power pills" that could release power into your life for the day, would you order yours quickly and take one diligently every day? Of course you would, and so would I. Guess what? God's words are power pills! Read what the apostle Paul wrote to the Hebrews:

> For the word of God is living and active and full of power [making it active, operative, energizing, and effective].
>
> Hebrews 4:12

I encourage you to spend thirty minutes a day studying God's Word, and I believe that after a while you will say that it has been life-changing!

Surround Yourself with the Right Friendships

Friendship is a powerful thing. And when you surround yourself with the right people, they can improve the quality of your life and make it one that is easy to love. Good friendships and healthy relationships make a major difference in each day—they make life a joy.

A British publication once offered a prize for the best definition of a friend. Among the thousands of answers received were the following:

- "One who multiplies joys, divides grief, and whose honesty is inviolable."
- "One who understands our silence."
- "A volume of sympathy bound in cloth."
- "A watch that beats true for all time and never runs down."

The winning definition read: "A friend is the one who comes in when the whole world has gone out."[21]

These are all wonderful definitions of what a positive, godly, encouraging friend can (and should) be in your life!

Unfortunately, not all the people we will encounter on a daily basis bring this kind of joy and understanding. If we are honest, we will realize there are many people who actually do more to make our lives difficult than anything else. Some people just have a complaining spirit, a propensity to gossip, or a negative outlook on life. It doesn't mean they are wicked or bad people, but it does mean they may be bad for you. It is not healthy to surround yourself with people who constantly bring you down.

I learned a long time ago that I needed to build an environment where I had access to positive, hope-filled people. My friends have an effect on me...and the same is true for you. We should be friendly to everyone we encounter, but wisdom tells us to use caution with the people that we habitually associate with. I'm not saying you should be guarded or skeptical of people. I'm encouraging you to ask God to give you wisdom when making close, personal friends. I ask God for what I call divine connections, people that He connects me with that He knows will be good for me.

> Ask God to give you wisdom when making close, personal friends.

We're not meant to go through life alone. Relationships are important. Surrounding yourself with encouragers and God followers is an essential part of loving your life. Helen Keller said, "I would rather walk with a friend in the dark than walk alone in the light."[22] In the Word of God we see that Philemon had a mentor (Paul), David had a group of friends referred to as the "mighty men," and even Jesus surrounded Himself with His group of disciples. Friendships and relationships are a very biblical idea—just make sure you are fostering an environment built on healthy, life-giving relationships.

If you have people in your own family or at your place of employment that are not godly, and who do not encourage you or anyone else, you may not be able to disassociate yourself from them. If that is the case, then it is especially important for you to have lots of friends and associates who provide the loving care you are not getting at home or at work. If you have one or two negatives influences in your life, but ten positive ones, the positives will win!

Choose Your Influences Carefully

There's an old saying that dates back to the very earliest days of computer programming: *Garbage in, garbage out.* It was meant to describe how a computer would respond to programming. If you put bad things into the computer, you would get bad results; conversely, if you wrote a good program, the computer would function wonderfully.

The same is true for our lives. What we put into our spirits will always affect how we live. What we think about, what we listen to, the things we read and watch—all of these influencers matter. They will help push us forward into God's plan or they will drag us back into defeat and frustration. The good news is this: We get to choose our influencers! We may not be able to choose every conversation we overhear or each piece of media we are bombarded with, but we *do* get to choose what we give a place of influence in our hearts.

Proverbs 4:23 (AMPC) says it this way: "Keep and guard your heart with all vigilance and above all that you guard, for out of it flow the springs of life."

In order to love our lives and move forward in God's plan for each of us, we must guard our hearts. We must protect them from the bitter, destructive influences of the world and fill our hearts with positive, life-giving things instead. I purposely choose as my close associates people who are easy to get along with, are encouraging, are positive, and pursue godly character. This helps me guard my heart. Here are a few ways to guard your heart today:

> In order to love our lives and move forward in God's plan for each of us, we must guard our hearts.

- Begin each day spending some time with the Lord in prayer. Ask Him to give you wisdom and discernment as to what you allow to influence your life that day.
- Turn off any media (television, radio, streaming services, etc.) that are giving you messages contrary to the Word of God. Don't allow the world to pour garbage into your soul.
- Listen to praise and worship music, or to good teaching that is based on the Bible throughout the day. This is an easy way to encourage your spirit...even while you're busy doing other things. You can listen to worship that glorifies God while you do your weekly grocery shopping, while you're waiting for the kids' soccer practice to be over, during your lunch break... pretty much anytime! There are so many great ways these days to access Christian music. It's much easier than in the days of the Walkman. (I can't tell you how many cassette tapes I wore out on that thing!)
- Unplug from any social media that leaves you feeling angry, frustrated, or bitter. In this digital age, there are so many social media options, and they can certainly be used for good things. (In my ministry, my team and I use social media quite often to encourage people with

God's Word.) However, as you probably know, a lot of social media is unhealthy. Whether it's people complaining about their lives, criticizing others, or just saying hurtful things, there are many ways social media sites can be a bad influence. Don't let those unhealthy influences sour your outlook on life. If you enjoy social media, then be sure to find encouraging, joy-filled social media friends who benefit you and add value to your life, rather than those who waste your time while draining you of joy.

As you go through your day today, be aware of your environment—the fish tank of your life. Is your tank clean? Is your water healthy? Are you swimming with compatible fish? If you will ask God to help you have the safest, healthiest environment for your life, He will do it! He wants the best for you, and it gives Him great pleasure to surround you with the very best. As you follow Him and seek His will, God will help you learn from His Word. He'll bring the right friends across your path and He will show you the best things to encourage your spirit. It is possible that one of the best things you can do for yourself right now is to get some new friends!

Don't Forget...

- In order to stay healthy (in your spirit, soul, and body) it is important that you develop a safe, clean, supportive environment around you.
- There is no better influence for your life than the Word of God—it is filled with His promises, instructions, and assurances of love for you.
- When you surround yourself with the right people, they can make loving life so much easier.
- What we put into our spirits will always affect how we live. What we think about, what we listen to, the things we read and watch—all of these influencers matter.

Change your thoughts and you can change your world.

Norman Vincent Peale

CHAPTER 18

Rediscover the Joy of Relationships

You can discover more about a person in an hour of play than in a year of conversation.

attributed to Plato

Have you ever noticed that the closer you are to something, the easier it is for that thing to lose its luster? We need to be very careful that we don't allow the extraordinary to become ordinary to us.

For example: The first time you visited the ocean, you were probably astounded at the beauty of the crashing waves. The wind in your hair and the sun on your face felt so good. You might have thought, *This is the greatest place on Earth!* But if you live near the ocean, it can become just another place. The more times you sit on the beach, the more commonplace it can become. I know people who live in ocean towns but never even go to the beach anymore.

Or what about the majesty of the mountains? If you vacation in a mountain town, you may be absolutely astounded by the beautiful mountains God created. You'd probably go hiking on mountain trails, attend tours in the local caves, and take a million selfies with the mountains in the background. But if you live there, you can easily lose that sense of awe. You may even begin to complain about the uneven terrain or the snowy winters.

Peace and quiet is another thing that we can lose our appreciation for. If you move away from a busy city to a nice, quiet town, you might love it at first. *Ah, this is nice. It's so peaceful here. This is the life!* But many times, that same "quiet life" you loved at first can turn into a boring life. Friends or family may visit you and say, "I love how quiet it is here," while you're thinking, *Really? I wish there were more things to do. Nothing stays open past 9:00 p.m.!*

Whether it's the ocean, the mountains, a small town, or any other number of things, it's incredibly easy to forget how great we have it.

Well, the same is true in relationships. It's very common for people to forget the things they once appreciated and enjoyed about their relationships. That marriage, that friendship, that family member that you were once so thankful for can become commonplace over the years. You used to think, *Wow! I'm so blessed to have this person in my life!* But now, you may be taking people for granted simply because you have become accustomed to having them in your life.

But in order to love your life, it is vital to enjoy, to value, and be grateful for the people God has given you. In order to do what I do in ministry, I need a lot of people to help me in a variety of ways. Very frequently when I am taking my morning walk, I thank God for

> It is vital to enjoy, to value, and be grateful for the people God has given you.

them, especially the ones who have helped me a long time. I don't want to take people for granted, because I don't want others to do that to me. It hurts when they do, and I don't want to be the source of that kind of pain for anyone else. Thanking God for them is my way of not allowing their extraordinary commitment to become common and ordinary to me.

And this is what God wants for you—the good relationships that you have are gifts from God, and He wants you to always remember that.

Look at these three verses in the Bible that talk about relationships:

> Now the Lord God said, It is not good (beneficial) for the man to be alone; I will make him a helper [one who balances him—a

counterpart who is] suitable and comple-
mentary for him.

Genesis 2:18

Now may the God who gives endurance
and who supplies encouragement grant that
you be of the same mind with one another
according to Christ Jesus.

Romans 15:5

Two are better than one because they have a
more satisfying return for their labor; for if
either of them falls, the one will lift up his
companion. But woe to him who is alone
when he falls and does not have another to
lift him up.

Ecclesiastes 4:9–10

These verses show us we were created to be in
healthy fellowship with others. God is a relational
God, and He wants us to discover (and rediscover)
the power and joy that comes with strong relationships. Whether it's marriage, a friendship, a family
bond—you can reap joy in your life by the simple
act of remembering how special the special people in
your life really are!

Rediscover Appreciation

One of the most dangerous things that can happen in a marriage is for two people to take each other for granted and lose their appreciation for one another. It's one of the biggest traps that can lead to divorce. *I love you! I can't live without you!* and *You are a blessing to me!* can turn into *Pick up your socks! Will you stop chewing so loudly? You need to be more aggressive!* And hundreds of other things we tend to complain about once a relationship is no longer valued as it should be. It's a pretty common occurrence and very sad to see.

But marriage isn't the only place this occurs. We can take our friends and our work associates for granted, our siblings for granted, our bosses for granted—the list goes on and on. But if you really want to have relationships that prosper and contribute to your life, today is the day you can rediscover your appreciation for those people—today is the day you can refuse to take them for granted.

Gratitude is a very biblical principle. First Thessalonians 5:18 says:

> In every situation [no matter what the circumstances], be thankful and continually give thanks to God, for this is the will of God for you in Christ Jesus.

When the apostle Paul was talking to his ministry partners, he said that he thanked God for them every time that he prayed (see Philippians 1:3–5). Apparently, Paul knew the value of the special people in his life, and we should follow his example.

> Gratitude not only improves your relationships, it improves you!

Gratitude not only improves your relationships, it improves you! If you'll be thankful for the people in your life who are a blessing to you as you go through your day, your heart will be glad and your relationships will grow stronger. Avoid the trap of taking people for granted—this will lead to boring, stale, and unhealthy relationships. Instead, have a grateful attitude and express that gratitude often.

One thing that prevents us from loving our lives is letting the extraordinary become ordinary, or, even worse, beginning to complain about things that we were at one time thankful for.

Rediscover a Servant's Heart

If you want to improve any relationship, start serving that person. Look for ways to meet their needs. Find things you can do to make their day easier. Schedule events that you know *they* will love, even if it's not your favorite thing to do. This is the heart of a servant, and it is an important key to rediscovering joy in your relationship. When you see their astonishment that you are going out of your way to bless *them*... you can't help but be blessed in return.

John 13:5 is one of the most incredible, mind-blowing Scriptures in the Bible. It says:

> Then He poured water into the basin and began washing the disciples' feet and wiping them with the towel which was tied around His waist.

What an unbelievable scene. Jesus, the very Son of God, served His disciples by washing their feet. If you think about it, every part of Jesus' ministry was about serving people out of His great love for them. Jesus never took anyone for granted. Paul said in Philippians 2:7 (AMPC) that Jesus "stripped Himself [of all privileges and rightful dignity], so as to assume the guise of a servant."

I believe that you and I should follow the example of Jesus today. Remember, any time you follow His example, good things take place. If you really want to love your life, follow the

> *Ask God how you can make other people happy and meet their needs.*

pattern Jesus, the Giver of life, set for us all. So instead of waiting for another person to make you happy or meet your needs, ask God how you can make them happy and meet their needs. I believe the only way we can avoid slipping into being greedy and unappreciative is to be aggressive about doing the things Jesus has instructed us to do.

Rediscover the Joy of Your Salvation

We have all kinds of different relationships in life, but the most important relationship you will ever have is your relationship with God. Your relationship with Him is the foundation for every other relationship you will have. That's why I think the best thing you can do to improve your relationships with others is to stay close to God and love Him more than you love anything or anyone else.

When asked what was the most important commandment, do you remember what Jesus said? In Mark 12:30–31, Jesus answered,

> And you shall love the Lord your God with all your heart, and with all your soul (life), and with all your mind...This is the second: You shall [unselfishly] love your neighbor as yourself.

I think the order there is very important—first we love God, and that gives us the capacity to love others.

Just as we can easily take people for granted, we can easily take God for granted. We can sometimes get so comfortable with Him (especially if we've been Christians for a while) that we stop developing our relationship with Him. Prayer decreases, Bible study gets set to the side, and we stop thanking Him for all His blessings. Let me encourage you today to avoid that trap. Take a moment and think of all God has done for you—He has saved you, He's delivered you, He has pulled you through times you never thought you could survive, and He loves you unconditionally.

He has prepared a place for you in Heaven where you will live in His presence for all eternity. Never take Him or any of His blessings for granted. Ask Him today to restore the joy of your salvation if you feel you need to, and don't wait for some magical feeling to come over you, but be aggressive in remembering and thanking Him for the most important relationship that you have—your relationship with God through Jesus Christ!

The Most (and Least) Important Words

In any relationship—with the Lord, our spouses, our children, our friends, or our coworkers—the words we say matter. This is true not only in relationships but in every part of our lives. What we say carries tremendous weight. That's why I want to share one last thing with you in this chapter about rediscovering the joy of relationships.

We've explored the importance of showing the people in our lives how much we value them. We've been reminded not to take others for granted, and of course, we've talked about the most important relationship of all—our relationship with God. But before we move on, I want to encourage you to tell those around you how much they mean to you. Two days ago, Dave told me how proud he is of me! He went on to name several things that I do that he really appreciates. It is not the first time Dave has done that, but I never get tired of hearing it. Don't hesitate to show appreciation with a note, a voice mail, a letter or card, or a phone call—or even better, do it in person when possible. Those words will be remembered for a long, long time, and they make the bond we have with others stronger each time we do it.

However you choose to communicate to those closest to you, let me share something I came across from an unknown source about the most (and least) important words you can share:

In any relationship, the SIX most important words you can say are:

"I admit I made a mistake."
The FIVE most important words:
"You did a good job."
The FOUR most important words:
"What do you think?"
The THREE most important words:
"After you, please."
The TWO most important words:
"Thank you."
The ONE most important word:
"We"
The LEAST important word:
"I"

I'm sure you can think of some other great words, too, but these are a great place to start. So go out today and see how they work! Share your heart, and your words, with someone important to you and watch their face light up with appreciation. When you do, it will help you rediscover they joy of that relationship and will greatly increase your capacity to love the life God has given you.

Don't Forget...

- Wake up each day and pray, "God, thank You so much for [name a special person in your life]. I'm truly happy to be in relationship with them!" It will help to keep the joy and wonder in that relationship from fading away.

- If you want to improve any relationship, start serving that person. Look for ways to meet their needs.
- Your relationship with God is the foundation for every other relationship you will ever have.
- Take a moment and think of all God has done for you—He has saved you, He's delivered you, He has pulled you through times you never thought you could survive, and He loves you unconditionally.

Peace begins with a smile.

Mother Teresa

CHAPTER 19

The Rewarding Result of Sacrifice

Remember that the happiest people are not those getting more, but those giving more.

H. Jackson Brown Jr.

There is a story told that Cyrus, the founder of the great Persian Empire, had once captured a foreign prince and the prince's entire family. When the prince was brought before him, Cyrus asked this prisoner of war, "What will you give me if I release you?" The prisoner, probably doubtful this would happen, replied, "I will give you half of all my vast wealth."

Unmoved, Cyrus then inquired, "What would you give me to release your children?" The prince replied, "For that, I would give you everything I possess."

The Persian emperor thought for a moment and then asked this question: "What will you give me to release your wife?" Without a moment's hesitation, the prisoner said, "Your Majesty, I will trade my life for hers. I will give myself." Cyrus was so incredibly moved by this answer that he decided to free the entire family.

As they traveled back to their home country, the prince said to his wife, "The legends of Cyrus are true. He was a powerful, handsome, and benevolent ruler." With love welling from her heart, his wife said, "I didn't notice. I could only keep my eyes on you— the one who was willing to give himself for me."[23]

This story illustrates something that is so true: Real love is about sacrifice. When you truly love a person, you are willing to sacrifice anything for them. Their safety, their happiness, their well-being, are more important than your own. You'll go to any lengths to meet their needs, even at great sacrifice to yourself. I think that is something we can all agree on—love is sacrifice, and sacrifice is love.

But when we talk about sacrifice, we naturally think it is a very painful thing. In fact, one of the definitions for the word "sacrifice" is "a loss so sustained."[24] We hear "sacrifice" and we assume work, discomfort, or pain. *I have to sacrifice my free time in order to be successful at work. I must sacrifice eating delicious desserts if I want to be thinner. Building muscle will require me to sacrifice for hours in the gym.* "Sacrifice" is often the image of blood, sweat, and tears.

While there is some truth to that notion (sacrifice

does require effort), I've discovered something about sacrifice that is rarely talked about—there is great joy in sacrificing yourself for others. Sacrifice isn't all about pain and discomfort. One of the best, most joyful, most rewarding things you'll ever do in life is make a personal sacrifice in order to enrich someone else's life.

I didn't always know this to be true. There was a time when I was too focused on myself to understand this biblical concept. But through the years, God has shown me that living to help others is one of the things that brings me the most happiness. It's a natural by-product. The more I try to help other people love their lives, the more I begin to love my own.

> *Make a personal sacrifice in order to enrich someone else's life.*

Hebrews 13:16 says,

> Do not neglect to do good, to contribute [to the needy of the church as expression of fellowship], for such sacrifices are always pleasing to God.

I know we all want to please God, so the fact that God is pleased when we sacrifice for someone else should immediately appeal to us. But there is an added benefit: It is pleasing to us, too! A life of sacrifice is a life you will truly begin to love.

Being willing to sacrifice for others doesn't mean that you will have no time left for yourself, or that your entire life needs to be sacrifice, sacrifice, and more sacrifice. God wants us to take care of ourselves, but He doesn't want us to be the center of our universe, living selfish and self-centered lives. The Holy Spirit will guide you in maintaining a balance in all areas of life if you become sensitive to His direction for you.

Compassion Is a Key to Happiness

There are many different facts of love, but one of the most important components to love is unselfishness. In the Bible, this is characterized as a willingness to sacrifice one's own wishes for those of others. Jesus is the ultimate example of this. He

> It's impossible to be happy and selfish at the same time.

sacrificed everything. He left His throne in Heaven to come to Earth. He spent His entire earthly ministry serving others, rather than being served. And He paid the ultimate sacrifice, giving His life for you and me. And it is His example that we should always strive to follow. The world tells us: *Get as much as you can* and *Look out for number one.* But Jesus modeled a much different attitude. The example He gave is a life that included sacrificing for others.

It's impossible to be happy and selfish at the same time. This is why God gives us the capacity to be *selfless.* It is in this selflessness that we find true peace and contentment. If we don't realize this, we will always struggle to be fulfilled. Selfish people are the center of their own lives, and it is difficult for them to learn and grow in God's plan for their lives, especially if it involves self-sacrifice (and it always does). A self-focused person expects everyone else to adjust to them and their needs. He or she simply doesn't know how to adapt to the needs of another without becoming angry or upset.

As I mentioned earlier, learning to adapt to others and make sacrifices for them was very difficult for me at one time in my life. I wanted my way, and I got upset when I didn't get it. I was selfish. I wanted what I wanted when I wanted it. I was not good at bending my own desires to accommodate someone else's timetable. A lot of my behavior problems were rooted in a fear of being controlled because my abusive father had controlled me. I thought as long as I stayed in control, I would be safe. But God wanted me to trust Him to keep me safe, rather than trying to do it myself.

Surely, I'm not the only one who has acted this way. Can you relate to that? Have you found yourself thinking about yourself all day long? *How is this situation going to affect me?! Why are these things happening to me?! I can't wait to get out of here so I can do what I want to do! Why isn't that person being more helpful to me?!* It's not that we're against other people—it's just that we are not focusing on them because we're too busy focusing on what we need, when we need it.

But what we fail to realize is that this focus on improving things for our own benefit doesn't actually improve anything at all. Instead, it leaves us feeling frustrated and bitter. All we can see is what we *don't* have and what people *aren't* doing for us. However, when we take our eyes off of ourselves and begin to look for ways to sacrifice for others, God comes in and meets our needs as we are joyfully working to meet the needs of other people.

In my life, God began to soften my heart, and I eventually learned to see the needs of others. I started to feel a compassion for them—the heartfelt desire to meet their needs before my own. Over time, I became more committed to walking in love. I learned to adapt my own desires in order to help meet the needs of others. There are still plenty of times in my life when I am selfish and God has to deal with me about it, but I rejoice that I'm not as selfish as I once was, and I trust God to continue helping me grow in being willing to sacrifice for others.

Not all people need the same things from us; everyone is different. Our children are a great example. One child may need more of our time while another needs more encouragement. Friends are the same way; their needs vary, and as we learn to walk in love and sacrifice for others we will seek to give them what they need rather than merely what is comfortable for us. Some parents make the mistake of buying their children something to show affection, when what children truly want is to spend time with them or to hear words spoken to them that will give them confidence. I encourage you to find out what your family and friends truly need and be willing to give it to them, even if it means that you need to sacrifice to do it.

Happiness comes with selflessness. You can never out-give God—the more you seek to bless His people, the more He blesses you in return. There will never be a day when you think, *I wish I hadn't been kind today* or *I really regret encouraging that friend earlier.* You will always go to bed happier when you take time during the day to sacrifice for someone else.

> There will never be a day when you think, I wish I hadn't been kind today.

Sacrificing for Others Doesn't Make You a Martyr

When we talk about sacrificing for others, sometimes people think that makes them a martyr. We've all heard about men and women, down through the ages, who paid the ultimate price and gave their lives for what they believed—they are martyrs. But there is another kind of martyr . . . one who is a self-inflicted martyr. This type of woe-is-me person lacks courage and nobility. They make sacrifices, but their heart is not right in doing so. They are actually sacrificing so they can feel good about themselves and ultimately brag about their many sacrifices.

You've probably met a person like this before (or maybe you've been this type of person at times). This person is willing to let everyone who will listen know all about their sacrifices and all they do for people. They want everyone to know how much they go through on a daily basis for the sake of others. They are exhausted and unhappy because they aren't sacrificing for the sheer joy of it—they are sacrificing for recognition.

I once knew a person like this. She felt like a slave to her family, and she definitely had the attitude of a martyr. All she talked about was how much she did for everyone and how little anyone appreciated her. In our conversations, it was obvious that she was keeping a running ledger of the work she was doing versus the reward she was receiving for it. Eventually, this attitude ruined many of her relationships.

Understand that the "martyr trap" is an easy one to fall into. If our motives aren't pure, we may start out serving our families and friends and loving it. But after a while, our hearts can begin to change and we begin to expect something in return. This isn't true, joyful sacrifice—this is manipulation. And it can happen unless we daily submit our heart and our motives to God. After all, we're working so hard and sacrificing a lot. This attitude can cause us to eventually lose the heart of a servant. We can become bitter because our expectations aren't being met. Our attitude sours, and we soon find out we've become mired in self-pity.

Whatever we do for others, we should do it in Jesus' name and in dependence upon Him (see Colossians 3:17), knowing that our reward will come from Him (see Colossians 3:23–24).

So as you embark on this journey to serve and sacrifice for the people in your life, ask God to help you do it with pure motives. Ask Him to show you how to love like He does, with a love that is unconditional and completely free. Let me give you one more illustration that I have a feeling you'll be able to identify with...

It's Not Always Easy, but It Is Always Worth It

I remember one day in particular when the Lord encouraged me to do something nice for Dave. I was going downstairs to make my morning coffee, and the Lord impressed on me something pretty simple in retrospect: Make a fruit salad for Dave. Sounds easy enough, right? Dave loves fruit salad in the morning, and I knew this would be a really nice thing to do for him. He wasn't up yet, so I knew I had more than enough time to prepare it for him and surprise him when he came downstairs.

There was one problem though: I didn't feel like making a fruit salad that day. I just didn't want to do it. I thought about how much time it would take to cut up all that fruit. I wanted to go pray and study my Bible instead! I wanted to do something I thought was *spiritual,* but the most spiritual thing I could really do at that moment was make the fruit salad with a good attitude.

I have to laugh about it now, because it's funny how we can make the mistake of thinking a spiritual activity, like praying or reading the Word of God, takes the place of obedience and makes us some sort of "super Christian"... because it does not. There is a right time for everything, and certainly there are times when we need to study and pray and refuse to get distracted by other things. But God put it on my heart to make the fruit salad, so that meant it was God's priority for me at that moment, and I could obey and still have plenty of time to study and pray.

As I thought about how much I really didn't want to make that fruit salad, the Lord patiently reminded me that this small sacrifice for Dave was actually more than serving my husband—it was service to God. So you can guess what I did. I obediently made the fruit salad and surprised Dave with it when he came downstairs that morning.

This was a very simple thing, but in God's eyes those kinds of things may be some of the greatest things. Little things may not be the things that people make a big deal over, but God sees them, and that is what is more important than anything else.

So look for little or big ways to sacrifice for someone else today. Give up your spot in line. Give a friend a ride. Mow someone's lawn. Smile. Share an encouragement. Or make a fruit salad! Whatever the sacrifice is, it never goes unnoticed by God!

Don't Forget...

- Real love is about sacrifice. When you truly love a person, you are willing to sacrifice anything for them.

- There is tremendous reward in sacrificing yourself for others.
- The world tells us: *Get as much as you can* and *Look out for number one*, but Jesus modeled a much different attitude. The example He gave is a life of loving sacrifice for others.
- It's impossible to be happy and selfish at the same time.
- Ask Jesus to show you how to love like He does, with a love that is unconditional and completely free.

AFTERWORD

I pray that you have not only enjoyed this book but that it will be used by God to help you learn to truly love your life. Your life is a gift from God, and loving your life is one of the best ways you can say "Thank You, Jesus." Your life, like mine, probably isn't and never will be perfect, but it is the only one you have, so embrace it and enjoy the adventure of doing life with God!

Let love be the center of your life! Love God with all your heart, soul, mind, and strength. Love yourself because Jesus loved you so much that He died for you. And love other people. The result will be that you will love your life!

Do you have a real relationship with Jesus?

God loves you! He created you to be a special, unique, one-of-a-kind individual, and He has a specific purpose and plan for your life. And through a personal relationship with your Creator—God—you can discover a way of life that will truly satisfy your soul.

No matter who you are, what you've done, or where you are in your life right now, God's love and grace are greater than your sin—your mistakes. Jesus willingly gave His life so you can receive forgiveness from God and have new life in Him. He's just waiting for you to invite Him to be your Savior and Lord.

If you are ready to commit your life to Jesus and follow Him, all you have to do is ask Him to forgive your sins and give you a fresh start in the life you are meant to live. Begin by praying this prayer...

Lord Jesus, thank You for giving Your life for me and forgiving me of my sins so I can have a personal relationship with You. I am sincerely sorry for the mistakes I've made, and I know I need You to help me live right.

Your Word says in Romans 10:9, "If you declare with your mouth, 'Jesus is Lord,' and believe in your heart that God raised him from the dead, you will be saved" (NIV). I believe You are the Son of God and confess You as my Savior and Lord. Take me just as I am, and work in my heart, making me the person You want me to be. I want to live for You, Jesus, and I am so grateful that You are giving me a fresh start in my new life with You today.

I love You, Jesus!

It's so amazing to know that God loves us so much! He wants to have a deep, intimate relationship with us that grows every day as we spend time with Him in prayer and Bible study. And we want to encourage you in your new life in Christ.

Please visit joycemeyer.org/salvation to request Joyce's book *A New Way of Living*, which is our gift to you. We also have other free resources online to help you make progress in pursuing everything God has for you.

Congratulations on your fresh start in your life in Christ! We hope to hear from you soon.

JOYCE MEYER MINISTRIES

U.S. & FOREIGN OFFICE
ADDRESSES

Joyce Meyer Ministries
P.O. Box 655
Fenton, MO 63026
USA
(636) 349-0303

Joyce Meyer Ministries—Canada
P.O. Box 7700
Vancouver, BC V6B 4E2
Canada
(800) 868-1002

Joyce Meyer Ministries—Australia
Locked Bag 77
Mansfield Delivery Centre
Queensland 4122
Australia
(07) 3349 1200

Joyce Meyer Ministries—England
P.O. Box 1549
Windsor SL4 1GT
United Kingdom
01753 831102

Joyce Meyer Ministries—South Africa
P.O. Box 5
Cape Town 8000
South Africa
(27) 21-701-1056

Teenagers Are People Too!
Trusting God Day by Day
The Word, the Name, the Blood
Woman to Woman
You Can Begin Again

JOYCE MEYER SPANISH TITLES

Belleza en Lugar de Cenizas (*Beauty for Ashes*)
Buena Salud, Buena Vida (*Good Health, Good Life*)
Cambia Tus Palabras, Cambia Tu Vida (*Change Your Words, Change Your Life*)
El Campo de Batalla de la Mente (*Battlefield of the Mind*)
Como Formar Buenos Habitos y Romper Malos Habitos (*Making Good Habits, Breaking Bad Habits*)
La Conexión de la Mente (*The Mind Connection*)
Dios No Está Enojado Contigo (*God Is Not Mad at You*)
La Dosis de Aprobación (*The Approval Fix*)
Empezando Tu Día Bien (*Starting Your Day Right*)
Hazte Un Favor a Ti Mismo…Perdona (*Do Yourself a Favor…Forgive*)
Madre Segura de sí Misma (*The Confident Mom*)
Pensamientos de Poder (*Power Thoughts*)
Sobrecarga (*Overload*)*
Termina Bien tu Día (*Ending Your Day Right*)
Usted Puede Comenzar de Nuevo (*You Can Begin Again*)
Viva Valientemente (*Living Courageously*)

* Study Guide available for this title

BOOKS BY DAVE MEYER

Life Lines

NOTES

1 https://www.goodreads.com/author/quotes/401826.John
_Flavel?page=3.

2 https://www.brainyquote.com/quotes/quotes/h/henrywardb121544
.html.

3 http://www.great-inspirational-quotes.com/i-would-pick-more
-daisies.html.

4 https://www.wsj.com/articles/SB10000872396390443989204577603341710975650.

5 http://www.goodreads.com/author/show/268402.Martha_Washington.

6 https://www.brainyquote.com/quotes/quotes/h/henrydavid108393
.html.

7 http://www.goodreads.com/quotes/69144-humor-is-mankind-s
-greatest-blessing.

8 http://ministry127.com/resources/illustration/this-is-the-time
-to-give.

9 https://quotefancy.com/quote/823157/Henri-J-M-Nouwen-To-give
-someone-a-blessing-is-the-most-significant-affirmation-we-can.

10 https://www.brainyquote.com/quotes/quotes/r/robertfros101059
.html?src=t_words.

11 Adapted from *Sower of Seeds*, FR. Brian Cavanaugh, Paulist Press, *Bits & Pieces*, June 22, 1995, pp. 2–3.

12 https://www.brainyquote.com/quotes/quotes/c/confucius134717
.html?src=t_life.

13 http://www.nydailynews.com/news/national/70-u-s-workers
-hate-job-poll-article-1.1381297.

14 https://www.brainyquote.com/quotes/quotes/k/kristinarm569046
.html?src=t_contentment.

15 https://bible.org/illustration/f-w-woolworth.

16 http://www.chrisreevehomepage.com/sp-dnc1996.html.

17 https://www.brainyquote.com/quotes/quotes/l/louiseboo170206
.html.

18 Reported in Deep Cove Crier, November 1993, Reporter Interactive
(umr.org), May 2001, and Tony Campolo, *Let Me Tell You a Story*;
https://storiesforpreaching.com/category/sermonillustrations/
gods-love/.

19 http://ministry127.com/resources/illustration/giving-away-what
-wasn-t-his.

20 Quoted in http://www.sermonillustrations.com/a-z/l/love.htm.

21 http://www.sermonillustrations.com/a-z/f/friendship.htm.

22 http://www.goodreads.com/quotes/tag/friendship.

23 http://www.sermonillustrations.com/a-z/s/sacrifice.htm.

24 http://www.thefreedictionary.com/sacrifice.